STRUCTURAL
REFORM IN
JAPAN

STRUCTURAL REFORM IN JAPAN

Breaking the Iron Triangle

 EISUKE SAKAKIBARA

BROOKINGS INSTITUTION PRESS
Washington, D.C.

Library of Congress Cataloging-in-Publication data

Sakakibara, Eisuke.
   Structural reform in Japan : breaking the iron triangle / Eisuke
Sakakibara.
   p. cm.
Includes index.
   ISBN 0-8157-7676-4 (cloth : alk. paper)
   1. Japan—Economic conditions—1989–   2. Japan—Economic policy—1989–
3. Japan—Social policy—1989–   4. Capitalism—Japan.   5. Banks and
banking—Japan.   I. Title.

   HC462.95.S228 2003
   330.952—dc22   2003018460

987654321

The paper used in this publication meets minimum requirements of the
American National Standard for Information Sciences—Permanence of Paper for
Printed Library Materials: ANSI Z39.48-1992.

Typeset in Adobe Garamond

Composition by R. Lynn Rivenbark
Macon, Georgia

Printed by R. R. Donnelley
Harrisonburg, Virginia

Contents

Preface to the English Edition   vii

Acknowledgments   xix

1 Collapse and Transformation   1

2 Japan's Modernization and Industrialization   12

3 Formation and Collapse
of the Public Construction State   23

4 From Structural Reform to Institutional Reform   38

5 Development of Global Corporations   58

6 The Japanese Banking System
and Its Nonperforming Loan Problem   70

7 Reopening Japan and Reforming
the Foreign Policy Regime   87

8 The Formation of the Japanese Meritocracy System   101

9 The Central versus Local Government Debate   111

10   Fundamental Change in Agricultural Policy   129

11   Health Care Reform   142

12   Building a New Nation   152

Index   161

Preface to the
English Edition

The events of the last decade that have led to the current recession have created intense, widespread interest in the Japanese economy or, more precisely, in the alleged failure of Japanese economic policy. This is probably due to similarities between the current economic situation in the U.S. and Europe and the Japanese experience. Paul Krugman, for example, states the following:

> The Japanese economy is encountering a long period of stagnation. It is plagued with a "liquidity trap" and "deflation," which developed economies have not experienced since the Depression of the 1930s. This should not be understood as a uniquely Japanese phenomenon. This is a problem that all developed economies could face. In particular, analysis of the Japanese recession is quite important for the U.S. economy. This is because the United States might one day experience what Japan has gone through during the last decade.[1]

1. Paul Krugman, *Kyōkō no Wana* (Tokyo: Chuōkōronsha, 2002), p. 5 (my translation).

Another indication of the high level of interest in this topic came from a leading Chinese government official. He commented to this author that China has been trying to learn from the "negative" lessons of Japanese policy management.

The popular view on this subject is that Japanese macro policies and financial supervision during the 1990s had been so poor that a bubble was created and then burst with the effects lingering on long afterward. Those having this viewpoint contend that the Bank of Japan (BOJ) had eased monetary policy excessively in the late 1980s due to external and internal political pressure. Then in the early 1990s, BOJ did the reverse by tightening its policy too aggressively, creating a prolonged deflationary pressure that has continued into the early twenty-first century. According to this popular view, the continuous and radical easing of monetary policy that was begun in the latter half of the 1990s, which led to a zero interest rate, was too late and too lukewarm in light of the extremely tight policy stance of the early 1990s.

A similar argument is made regarding fiscal policy. The contention is that the fiscal packages formulated and implemented almost every year during the decade were too little and too late.

Indeed, timing and public relations are important in macro policies and the performance of Japanese authorities has been very poor on both counts. However, it is still hard to believe that monetary policy leading to a zero interest rate and continuous quantitative easing and fiscal policy resulting in accumulated debt of over 150 percent of GDP have not had at least some impact on the macroeconomy. This paradox suggests that the problems that have plagued the Japanese economy may be structural rather than cyclical.

Causes of Stagnation

My analysis suggests that the major cause of the decade-long stagnation of the Japanese economy was the lack of profitable investment opportunities due to a high cost structure rather than weak consumption or residential construction caused by high real interest rates or a lack of credit. In other words, the problem was on the IS curve, particularly investment demand, and not on the LM curve.[2] A continuing decline in investment demand

2. The IS (investment-saving) curve represents the equilibrium of the goods and services market (demand for goods equals the supply of goods) for all combinations of real income and the real inter-

shifted the IS curve leftward resulting in low GDP growth despite a right-ward shift of the LM curve caused by the increase in the money supply pushing the real interest rate down. This phenomenon can be explained as follows.

For the first time since World War II, plant and equipment investment declined extensively in real terms year-on-year for six out of the twelve years from 1991 through 2002. One of the causes of this abnormal decline, as pointed out by Masaru Yoshitomi, was a reaction to the excessive investment of the late 1980s. There were, however, other factors that were structural in nature.[3]

Japanese corporate earnings suffered a marked decline in the 1990s while real wages increased. The net income of Japanese corporations in 1998 was only 64.2 percent of that in 1990 and the aggregate net income of all corporations listed on the First Section of the Tokyo Stock Exchange was negative. At the same time, real wages jumped from an index of 95.2 in 1990 (1995 = 100) to 103.8 in 1999. As a share of GDP, wages and salaries increased from 57.3 percent in 1990 to 61.4 percent in 1999, contrasted with a decline in corporate income from 11.3 percent of GDP in 1990 to 10.8 percent in 1999. These shifts in wages and corporate earnings were in opposition to those in the United States, where real wages remained relatively unchanged (an index of 102.1 in 1990 versus 102.8 in 1999) and corporate income increased (from 5.2 percent of GDP in 1990 to 6.5 percent in 1999).

Costs for Japanese corporations were pushed up not only by wages. The efficiency level of the construction, distribution, transportation, and other domestic industries deteriorated during the 1990s. The level of productivity of domestic manufacturing and service industries was estimated to be less than two-thirds that of their U.S. counterparts.[4] For example, productivity in the construction industry declined at the annual rate of 3 percent

---

est rate. The LM (liquidity-money) curve represents the equilibrium of the money market (real money demand equals real money supply) for all combinations of real income and the real interest rate. At the point where the IS and LM curves intersect is the equilibrium point for both the goods market and the money market.

3. Masaru Yoshitomi, "Nihon Keizai no Shinjitsu" (Tokyo: Tōyō Kēzai Shinpōsha, 1998) (my translation).

4. McKinsey Global Institute, *Why the Japanese Economy Is Not Growing: Micro Barriers to Productivity Growth* (Washington, 2000), Executive Summary, pp. 1–5.

during the 1990s while the number of employees in the industry increased by as much as 670,000 during the same period.

> Since this sector employs more than 10 per cent of industrial work-ers, the average annual decline of productivity by 3 per cent in the 1990s had a large impact on productivity growth of industry. The substantial increase in public works and the inclination by banks to maintain credit lines and to forgive debt, even for inefficient firms, allowed the construction sector to absorb 670 thousand workers between 1990 and 1999 despite a sharp drop of its value added over the same period.[5]

Despite an environment of overall deflation, the high cost structure of the Japanese economy had worsened, and it was only natural that export-oriented manufacturing firms competing in global markets had started to relocate their production bases outside of Japan, with China being a major destination. If service sectors such as medical care and distribution or domestic manufacturing sectors such as food processing had been deregu-lated, investments in Japan would have increased in those sectors. Those sectors had been politicized and strongly protected by regulations and sub-sidies, however. Thus, it was only natural that plant and equipment in-vestments declined in the 1990s because of very limited opportunities to start profitable domestic ventures. In my estimation, therefore, this lack of investment opportunities caused by the high cost structure is the major rea-son the Japanese economy has remained stagnant for the last ten years.

It is true that the nonperforming asset problem has been one reason that bank lending continued to decline despite monetary easing; however, the rapid reduction in corporate investment and loan demand has been a much more important reason. With export-oriented manufacturers shift-ing their production away from Japan and with the high barrier to entry in domestic manufacturing and services, it is only natural that demand for loans and other financial resources is stagnating.

It is, therefore, quite reasonable to conclude that the primary cause of the decade-long stagnation of the Japanese economy was not the conduct of macro policies but rather the weakening of the revenue structure of Japanese corporations within a "socialistic" policy regime where progress on reforms has been very slow.

5. OECD, *OECD Economic Surveys: Japan 2001* (Paris: OECD, November 2001), p. 39.

Failure to Break the "Iron Triangle"

What should be criticized here is not the way in which monetary and fiscal policies were implemented but rather the inability of Japanese leadership to break the iron triangle made up of the Liberal Democratic Party (LDP), the bureaucracy, and vested interest groups. The point has been reached where the need for structural reform to revitalize the economy is urgent. The popular view on structural reform, particularly in the U.S., is limited in scope and naive in the sense that it advocates the adoption of a universal model for a market economy, irrespective of historical legacy and culture. This perspective often focuses on the problem of nonperforming assets, with the solution offered being their quick disposition along with consolidation of the banking sector. The financial supervision of banks by the Ministry of Finance during the 1990s has often been cited as a major obstacle to such reform, although some changes have been made since the establishment of the Financial Services Agency (FSA) as an entity independent of the Ministry of Finance.

Although I do not necessarily disagree with the points raised by analysts regarding the collapse of the "convoy system" of financial supervision, I would like to point out that this system was simply part of a much broader policy regime which in this book I label the "party-bureaucracy complex." It is true that the *ancien régime* encompassing the LDP, the Ministry of Finance, the Ministry of Economy, Trade and Industry, and others has become dysfunctional and that the nonperforming asset problem is one of the major symptoms of its failure. But in this context two things need to be emphasized.

First, as I have already indicated, it is not simply that macro policies and financial supervision have failed the economy, but rather that the whole structure or institution has become dysfunctional. This author's definition of structure is somewhat different from that often used by orthodox macroeconomists. In my usage, the concept of "structure" is interchangeable with that of "institutions." My notion of "institutions" or "structure" is the same as that of Masahiko Aoki or Douglass C. North, which is in essence "an equilibrium of self-enforcing rules of the game."[6] There are multiple equilibria for any given environment or set of external factors. Therefore, in any given environment it is possible for a Japanese equilibrium to be different from a U.S. equilibrium. In other words, there is no

6. Masahiko Aoki, *Toward a Comparative Institutional Analysis* (MIT Press, 2001), pp. 10–11.

unique or universal equilibrium. Of course, structure or institution does evolve over time and, under certain circumstances, different structures or institutions can converge.

Second, the time dimension is quite important here. The "old" Japanese institution or structure functioned well up to the early 1980s, and it was the change in environment that subsequently rendered that institution or structure obsolete. In a timeless model of neoclassical economics, there may be an optimal (or Pareto-optimal) system, but the real world is more dynamic than this simple model allows and its application for policymaking is not justifiable.

In 1990 I published the book *Beyond Capitalism,* wherein I described the Japanese politico-economic system as a dual structure consisting of a large corporate sector and a public sector.[7] This model of a blended economy, it was argued, is quite different from America's market economy, but it functioned quite effectively in the past. In this book, thirteen years later, I contend that this same "dual" system has become dysfunctional and that major structural or institution reform is necessary. (Although I briefly touched upon the need for structural reform in the last part of the previous publication, I argued at that time for some structural adjustments essentially to preserve the basic tenets of the old system.)

The Roles of Government and the Market

Why the apparent change in my opinion? Have I fundamentally changed my view on the market economy or the role of government? I do not deny that thirteen years is a long time and my thinking has evolved significantly over that period.

In my view, there have been two major environmental changes during the course of the last decade or so. They are path-breaking technological innovations that could be considered the third industrial revolution and the globalization of countries like China and India. In chapter 1 of this book, I propound these two phenomena as the motivating factors behind the great transformation of the world economy and social system. Japan's blended economy that generally functioned quite well from just after the Meiji Restoration up through the 1970s or 1980s has become gradually

7. Eisuke Sakakibara, *Beyond Capitalism: The Japanese Model of Market Economics* (Lanham, Md.: University Press of America; Economic Strategy Institute, 1993). The original Japanese version was published in 1990.

dysfunctional as the technological revolution and globalization accelerate and spread around the world.

Past success is often a major reason for current failure. Because of the remarkable success of the past, Japan has had enormous difficulty changing its current institution or structure. The rules of the game have started to change, a new equilibrium has not yet been reached, and the old regime still dominates the system.

According to Aoki, "the search for new rules of the game, or a new institution, started in 1993 in the political arena when the one-party dominance of the LDP ended."[8] The ten-year period between 1993 and the current Koizumi Government could be viewed as the first act of Japanese structural or institutional reform. Prime Minister Koizumi may be now (in 2003) closing the curtain on the first act. In hindsight, these first ten years of reform were the period when partial reforms were slowly implemented within the constraints of the party-bureaucracy complex, or the rule of the iron triangle centered on the LDP. Some meaningful structural reform, such as the financial Big Bang and deregulation in various areas were implemented, although belatedly or slowly.[9]

What Koizumi has demonstrated to the general public and the rest of the world is that further structural reforms are extremely difficult to implement as long as the party-bureaucracy complex dominates decisionmaking. Unlike some naive economists, this author does not think that economic policies can be formed and implemented independently of the political regime. Institutional or structural reform can only be achieved when both economic and political institutions change. In this sense, Japan may now be entering the second act of structural reform, which would involve a major change in the political regime. The second act, which could be much more radical than the first, will likely last for five to ten years.

Thus, my notion of structural or institutional reform is much broader than that of the majority of economists. In this book I try to cover not only the nonperforming asset problem but also broad issues in such sectors as

8. Masahiko Aoki, *Utsuriyuku Kono Jūnen Ugokanu Shiten* (Tokyo: Nikkei Business Bunko, 2002), p. 368 (my translation).

9. In November 1996, Prime Minister Hashimoto initiated extensive financial system reform that was called the Japanese version of the Big Bang. The goal of this reform was to revitalize the Japanese financial market commensurate with those of New York and London by 2001. Two major elements of the Big Bang to be carried out in tandem were (1) reform that encompassed the principles of liberalization, fairness, and globalization and (2) the disposal of the nonperforming loans of financial institutions. For further details see www.mof.go.jp.

education, agriculture, and medical care. Because of the limitations of time and space, I may not have covered each area comprehensively or as deeply as possible. The point of including them is that I would like readers to note that structural reform includes not simply changes in bank supervision or the deregulation of specific industries. It could even be said that what is required is a social and economic revolution that in historical cases has taken as much as two to three decades to complete. The task, perhaps, is comparable to the Meiji Restoration of the late nineteenth century that laid the foundation for Japanese modernization and industrialization.

This restoration process was by no means smooth and orderly. Although the current situation is different, the institutional or structural change required is just as challenging and difficult as that of the Meiji Restoration.

The Challenge of Structural Reform

Let us take the example of the nonperforming asset problem to illustrate the complexity or challenge of the structural reform we are facing. This problem is often compared to the U.S. financial crisis of the late 1980s and 1990s. The Japanese situation is much deeper than, and qualitatively different from, the U.S. case, however. The level of debt vis-à-vis capital or operating profit is extremely high in Japan's case—even after the bursting of the bubble and the decade-long recession. Second, the proportion of bank financing, or indirect financing, is much higher in Japan. For example, in the U.S. the level of outstanding loans of banks and other financial institutions hovered around 40 percent during the 1980s and 1990s, whereas in Japan it was as high as 93 percent in 2000. The worst nonperforming asset ratio for the U.S. was 5.4 percent in 1991 while for Japan it was 15 percent or even higher. Another major difference is that Japan has been suffering from a decade of debt deflation, or a continuous decline in asset prices, that has no prospect of bottoming out in the near future.

Thus, the U.S. experience in resolving its financial crisis of a decade ago would by no means be an appropriate role model for Japanese policy in the area of nonperforming asset disposition. The nationalization or bankruptcy of one or two city banks along with the restructuring of 30 to 40 big corporations in construction, distribution, and other industries would not by itself solve the problem, which is much too deep and widely spread for that to be successful. Excessive debt and nonperforming assets are much larger for small and medium-sized enterprises (SMEs) and local financial institutions, respectively, than for large corporations and institutions. This is a significant fact given that in Japan 97 percent of corporations are SMEs. The debt–cash flow ratio for SMEs in 2002 was as high as 36.2 compared to 18.3 for large corporations. Thus, unless the excessive debts of SMEs and nonperforming assets of local banks and other financial institutions are dealt with, Japan's financial system cannot be successfully restructured and revitalized.

Behind this excessive debt and nonperforming asset problem lurks deflation, which is an apparent structural problem. Price deflation for goods and services is unfortunately combined with continuous asset price deflation in Japan, creating a situation similar to that of the U.S. in the 1930s. Although I do not intend to take up the discussion here of whether deflation is a structural issue or just a monetary phenomenon, I would like to note that the great transformation of the world economy, characterized by the third industrial revolution and globalization, is behind this structural deflation.[10]

Many U.S. and European economists still contend that deflation is not global but is a uniquely Japanese phenomenon. However, both historical and recent data indicate that position has become increasingly indefensible. First, it is clear at least that disinflation has accelerated in the last decade or so. The increase in the consumer price index (CPI) had been greater than 5 percent in 23 developed countries up to the early 1980s but slowed to around 3 percent during the 1980s. By the end of the 1990s, the increase was down to about 2 percent. Data for 2001–02 show that four economies (Japan, China, Singapore, and Hong Kong) experienced a decline in the CPI, and in addition to these four economies, Indonesia, Taiwan, the Philippines, Canada, Germany, the United States, Italy, and France reported a decline in the wholesale price index.

Although the recent gyration in the price of oil, which is related to the current geopolitical situation, masks this trend, it is difficult to argue that these nearly two decades of disinflation are a cyclical phenomenon. It cannot be concluded yet from the data that deflation is both global and structural, but it is a good possibility that countries like Japan and China are just ahead of the U.S. and Europe in experiencing this phenomenon. For certain service sectors, such as medical care, or for certain commodities where the supply is physically limited (for example, oil), deflation may not take place. For most manufactured goods and certain services where production

10. For a detailed discussion of structural deflation, see Eisuke Sakakibara, *Kōzō Defure no Seiki (Century of Structural Deflation)* (Tokyo: Chuōkōronsha, 2003) (available only in Japanese).

in, or outsourcing to, countries like China and India is possible, however, deflation will continue for some sustained period of time.

Thus, even the resolution of the nonperforming asset problem is extremely complicated in a deflationary environment for goods and services and cannot be dealt with separately from other policies. How do we deal with the issue of corporate governance for SMEs? How do we change relationship banking in local communities? How do we deal with asset price deflation, which is still continuing?

What complicates any genuine structural or institutional reform is that institutions complement one another, and changing the rules of the game within the limits of a single sector is, therefore, sometimes impossible. Reforms need to be implemented simultaneously across many sectors even though the reforms have to be partial. Fan Gang refers to China's structural reform program as "Parallel Partial Progression" (PPP),[11] which was quite successful in China during the last decade.[12] (This success should be compared to the failure of the shock-therapy policy carried out in Russia during the same period.)

Simultaneous vs. Sector Reform

What Japan needs is not shock therapy (à la Takenaka) for the resolution of nonperforming assets, but rather more widely scoped PPP in various areas of Japan's economic and political structure. The goal of this book is to present a rough sketch of the areas where genuine structural or institutional reform should be simultaneously implemented in order to achieve overall success for the Japanese economy.

Readers, particularly specialists in the Japanese economy, may wonder why I venture into such diverse areas as diplomacy, education, agriculture, and medical services, none of which seem to have direct links to the Japanese economy or even to macroeconomic issues. However, structural reforms by definition are sector specific in nature, and the complementary

11. Fan Gang's parallel partial progression is an approach to reform for countries in transition like China. PPP is a gradual approach that has two key elements: reform should be undertaken in all institutions simultaneously rather than sequentially, and compatibility should be maintained throughout so that the various steps promote and facilitate one another and chaos is avoided.

12. Fan Gang, "'Sequencing' or 'Parallel Partial Progression': A Note on Approaches to Transition and Case of China," NERI Working Paper 035 (Beijing: National Economic Research Institute, China Reform Foundation, 2002).

nature of institutions or structure requires the simultaneous treatment of politics and economics along with the various sectors of Japanese society.

I admit that the problem is of such depth and wide scope that the rough sketch presented in this book needs to be expanded in each of the areas covered. However, it is hoped that the book furthers the understanding that structural reform or new institution-building in Japan needs an all-encompassing approach that includes the various sectors of Japanese society and the economy. Only with this kind of understanding can one implement pragmatic and meaningful structural reform in Japan.

Acknowledgments

My work on the English translation of this book began in September 2001 while I was a visiting fellow at the Paul H. Nitze School of Advanced International Studies (SAIS) of the Johns Hopkins University in Washington, D.C. I am deeply indebted to Professors Karl Jackson and Frederick Brown of SAIS for their kind advice and guidance at that time. I am also very grateful to Dr. John Langlois and the Center for International Political Economy (CIPE) in New York for giving me a research grant to conduct analysis and give lectures at SAIS on structural reform of the Japanese economy.

Ms. Kanae Watanabe-Kaye worked as my assistant while I was at SAIS and translated the original Japanese book into English. Ms. Sharon Yamakawa then refined the translation in consultation with the author and the publisher. I owe a great deal to both of them for the final product. Since the original book was intended for the Japanese audience, the refining and editing of the translation for non-Japanese readers was quite difficult. Without the assistance of Ms. Yamakawa, the task could not have been accomplished so well in such a short period of time.

STRUCTURAL
REFORM IN
JAPAN

1 Collapse and Transformation

The rapid advance of globalization, which began at the end of the twentieth century, continues to dramatically change the world in which we live. While fostering democracy and the expansion of markets, globalization is also causing the collapse and transformation of the twentieth century system.

Both Akihiko Tanaka and Nobuo Noda interpret this phenomenon as the weakening of the nation state and define it as the advent of a new "Middle Ages" in the twenty-first century. Tanaka states that the world in the twenty-first century will experience the waning of the nation state and the rise of competing actors, such as corporations and nongovernmental organizations (NGOs). At the same time, liberal democracy will stand out and endure as "the ideology"—from among the various ideologies of the twentieth century, including socialism and fascism—as Christianity did in Europe during the Middle Ages.

While Tanaka foresees the recurrence of the Middle Ages because of the abiding nature of American values and order, Noda rather sees a Huntington-type "clash of civilizations" with the arrival of an "imperial" era.[1] Referring to Jean-Marie Guéhenno's *End of the Nation State,* Noda states the following:

> With the development of borderless-ness, the state, the very concept of which is inseparable from its borders, will inevitably decline. Over time, the world will become a collection of networks that have nothing to do with territory. Guéhenno goes on to predict that the political institutions suitable for these conditions will be vague "empires without emperors."[2]

Noda predicts the resurgence of a Chinese empire alongside the United States, Russia, and Central Europe (a European empire centered around Germany). In this context, he says that Japan "must solidify a wide-reaching order to assure its position."[3] Certainly, "middle aging" due to globalization, as Tanaka and Noda suggest, is possible. However, I do not think there will be a definitive ideology in the twenty-first century, as proposed by Tanaka. As explained later, this is because the forces of economic liberalism and democracy lead in completely opposite directions. Although these forces were reconciled in the post–World War II period by the social democratic welfare policy of the state, in the rapid flow of globalization this compromise is about to collapse. Noda's prediction of the formation of small regional empires, as opposed to states, which have various ethnic values in common, seems to be a possibility. One wonders if the momentum of the trends toward erosion of borders and the expansion of markets will continue at the current rate and if the state will indeed fade away.

Comparison with Globalization under *Pax Britannica*

The current trend of globalization is similar to that of globalization during 1870 to 1913 under *Pax Britannica.* The two waves of globalization, which are a century apart, are not exactly the same, however; if the first is "classical globalization," then the latter could be called "neoclassical globalization." John Maynard Keynes, in his 1920 book *The Economic Consequences of the Peace,* looked back on this classical period with nostalgia:

1. Samuel Huntington, "The Clash of Civilizations?" *Foreign Affairs,* vol. 7, no. 3 (1993), pp. 22–49.
2. Nobuo Noda, *Nijusseki o dō Miruka* (Tokyo: Bunshun Shinsho, 1994), p. 125 (my translation).
3. Noda, *Nijusseki o dō Miruka,* p. 219 (my translation).

What an extraordinary episode in the economic progress of man that age was which came to an end in August, 1914! . . . The inhabitant of London could order by telephone, sipping his morning tea in bed, the various products of the whole earth, in such quantity as he might see fit, and reasonably expect their early delivery upon his doorstep; he could at the same moment and by the same means adventure his wealth in the natural resources and new enterprises of any quarter of the world, and share, without exertion or even trouble, in their prospective fruits and advantages; or he could decide to couple the security of his fortunes with the good faith of the townspeople of any substantial municipality in any continent that fancy or information might recommend.[4]

During that time, the United Kingdom's 8 to 9 percent average current account surplus was used mainly to invest in public and corporate bonds that recycled money to the New World. It is thought that the direct investment and securities investment by the United Kingdom in the 1910s was as high as 180 percent of GDP. This far outweighs the net overseas assets of the current largest creditor nation, Japan (60 percent of GDP in 1998) and of the current largest debtor nation, the United States (68 percent of GDP in 1998). During this time, not only the United Kingdom but also European nations such as France and Germany invested heavily in the United States, Canada, Argentina, Australia, and other countries. Although the real GDP growth rate of the United Kingdom from 1870 to 1913 is estimated to have been less than 2 percent, that of countries like the United States and Canada was over 4 percent. By the beginning of the twentieth century, Argentina had already joined the developed nations by achieving 6.4 percent average growth.

As is the case now, the rapid development of transportation and communications technology supported globalization at that time. The rapid progress in the development of railroads, shipping, and automobiles, along with the telephone and telegraph, greatly affected economic activity.

World War I, however, brought a sudden end to this era of globalization. The world entered a period of depression and protectionism. Keynes pointed out the weakness of globalization, which at that time was seen as

---

4. John Maynard Keynes, *The Economic Consequences of the Peace* (New York: Harcourt, Brace and Howe, 1920), p. 11.

inevitable.[5] What we must consider now is whether these historical lessons are relevant to the current wave of globalization.

In 1997 the progress of capital liberalization, which was driven by both the information technology (IT) revolution and globalization, plunged East Asia into economic turmoil. By the fall of 1998 it had involved Wall Street, pushing events to the brink of a global capital crisis. Fortunately, the successful financial policies of the United States, combined with the global increase in IT-related infrastructure investment, temporarily avoided a massive crisis.

During the crisis of 1998 George Soros in his book entitled *The Crisis of Global Capitalism* forecast the same fate for the current wave of extreme globalization, specifically market fundamentalism, as that of the globalization period from 1870 to 1913. "Financial markets are inherently unstable and there are social needs that cannot be met by giving market forces free rein," the author states. "It is market fundamentalism that has rendered the global capitalist system unsound and unsustainable."[6] While Soros is not saying that globalization itself will lead to collapse, he is saying the fundamentalist paradigm that relies too much on the market will inevitably collapse.

Dani Rodrik suggests that an undeniable contradiction exists between democracy and a completely free market.[7] To coexist, the global market must be supported by the state through public policy. As noted earlier, from the end of World War II through the 1980s, many governments around the world implemented social welfare policies that prevented the actualization of this contradiction. However, the rapid technological innovation and the accompanying structural reforms of the 1980s and 1990s are now bringing the contradiction between the global market and democracy to the surface.

We should, therefore, consider whether the rapid progress of globalization in the current era is different in nature from that under *Pax Britannica*. Although unmistakable points of similarity can be found, it is also clear that the prior globalization based on industrialization and modernization

5. Keynes, *Economic Consequences of the Peace.*

6. George Soros, *The Crisis of Global Capitalism: Open Society Endangered* (New York: Public Affairs, 1998), p. xx.

7. Dani Rodrik, "The Debate over Globalization: How to Move Forward by Looking Backward," paper presented at the conference on "The Future of World Trading System," Institute of International Economics, Washington, 1998.

is very different from the current globalization based on the information revolution, growth of the service sector, and postmodernism.

The Birth of Network Globalization

In his recent book, Francis Fukuyama describes the beginning of the era of *The Great Disruption*:

> Over the past half-century, the United States and other economically advanced countries have gradually made the shift into what has been called an "information society," the "information age," or the "post-industrial era." Futurist Alvin Toffler has labeled this transition the "Third Wave," suggesting that it will ultimately be as consequential as the two previous waves in human history: from hunter-gatherer to agricultural societies and then from agricultural to industrial ones.
>
> This shift consists of a number of related elements. In the economy, services increasingly displace manufacturing as a source of wealth. Instead of working in a steel mill or automobile factory, the typical worker in an information society has a job in a bank, software firm, restaurant, university, or social service agency. The role of information and intelligence, embodied in both people and increasingly smart machines, becomes pervasive, and mental labor tends to replace physical labor. Production is globalized as inexpensive information technology makes it increasingly easy to move information across national borders, and rapid communications by television, radio, fax, and e-mail erodes the boundaries of long-established cultural communities.[8]

Although greater ease of transportation and communication also played an important role in the nineteenth century process of globalization, this time, the revolutionary technological advances, such as major increases in the power of the computer and the Internet, have made it possible for people to communicate at almost no cost to the individual. Thomas Friedman, in his book *The Lexus and the Olive Tree*, writes about his 79-year-old mother playing bridge over the Internet with three Frenchmen in 1998:

---

8. Francis Fukuyama, *The Great Disruption: Human Nature and the Reconstitution of Social Order* (Touchstone, Simon and Schuster, 1999), p. 3.

There are some things about this new era of globalization that we've seen before (but which are much more intense now), some things that we've never seen before and some things that are so new we don't even understand them yet. For all these reasons, I would sum up the differences between the two eras of globalization this way: If the first era of globalization shrank the world from a size "large" to a size "medium," this era of globalization is shrinking the world from a size "medium" to a size "small."[9]

The Differences from the Past

As typified by Friedman's mother, globalization currently is a network-type structure in which the masses can participate. Those who participated in the globalization that took place from the nineteenth century through the beginning of the twentieth century were essentially the elite. Furthermore, the process of globalization itself was imposed from above by the hegemonic United Kingdom. It was not something in which the New World railroad workers, for example, were involved. The structure at that time could be called *hierarchical* globalization, while the current structure could be differentiated as *network* globalization.

Another characteristic of network globalization is that the participation in financial and currency markets has expanded from a segment of society made up of financial institutions and wealthy individual investors to one that also includes universities, foundations, and individuals, among other players. This broadening of participants in the market also includes not only developed nations and particular nations that are the recipients of investment, but also most countries, with the exception of the poorest. In the 1990s particularly, financial and currency transactions were liberalized in developing nations, and what was previously *current-account* globalization is now becoming *capital-account* globalization. This network globalization has gradually begun to alter, and in some cases destroy, the modern systems and institutions of the era of industrialization, first in the United States, then in the rest of the world, primarily in other developed countries. On this issue, Francis Fukuyama said:

Certainly many of the benefits of an information society are clear, but have all of its consequences necessarily been so positive? People asso-

9. Thomas Friedman, *The Lexus and the Olive Tree* (HarperCollins, 2000), p. xix.

ciate the information age with the advent of the Internet in the 1990s, but the shift away from the Industrial era started more than a generation earlier with the de-industrialization of the Rust Belt in the United States and comparable moves away from manufacturing in other industrialized countries. This period, from roughly the mid-1960s to the early 1990s, was also marked by seriously deteriorating social conditions in most of the industrialized world. Crime and social disorder began to rise, making inner-city areas of the wealthiest societies on earth almost uninhabitable. The decline of kinship as a social institution, which has been going on for more than two hundred years, accelerated sharply in the last half of the twentieth century. Fertility in most European countries and Japan fell to such low levels that these societies will depopulate themselves in the next century, absent substantial immigration; marriages and births became fewer; divorce soared; and out-of-wedlock childbearing came to affect one out of every three children born in the United States and over half of all children in Scandinavia. Finally, trust and confidence in institutions went into a deep, forty-year decline. A majority of people in the United States and Europe expressed confidence in their governments and fellow citizens during the late 1950s; only a small minority did so by the early 1990s. The nature of people's involvement with one another changed as well. Although there is no evidence that people associated with each other less, their mutual ties tended to be less permanent, less engaged, and with smaller groups of people. These changes were dramatic, they occurred over a wide range of similar countries, and they all appeared at roughly the same period in history. As such, they constituted a Great Disruption in the social values that prevailed in the industrial age society of the mid-twentieth century.[10]

Network globalization's effect on interpersonal relationships as well as on social structure has led to the destruction of the old order. At this point, the nature of the new system and its values are not clear; nor is it known how the contradiction between the global market and democracy, mentioned by Rodrik, will be resolved.

It has become more and more difficult for Europe and Japan to continue along the social welfare track, because of globalization. Although the social democratic parties in Europe have started down a third path combining

---

10. Fukuyama, *The Great Disruption,* pp. 4–5.

global markets with welfare in a new way, no one can predict what kind of society this "third path" will lead to.

The European Union as the Third Path

Jacques Attali concedes the dominance of market principles and democracy under the new globalization. While rejecting its universality, he foresees a new third path in the liberal European Union's acceptance of multilateralism.

> With the end of Communism, progressive universalism has collapsed. In other words, Europe's last imperial attempt to push "one set of laws" on the world, which promised a bright future to those who tried to implement it, has ended in failure. Already in Europe, there are only the two values left—market principles and democracy. It is true that, according to many, market principles and democracy are still a universal "set of laws." However, these two values cannot fulfill humanity's dreams of universality, eternity, and a path to utopia that are implied by the "set of laws. Because market principles and democracy are based on something temporary and fluctuating, their foundation is weak. They cannot attain the justice or timelessness that humans need to exist because both of them reject eternity and memory, while emphasizing the moment and forgetting. In other words, neither market principles nor democracy can create a "set of laws" that should be applied worldwide, nor can they guarantee a future.[11]

In this way, Attali rejects market principles and democracy as universal values and offers the unification of Europe as the cause for European nations.

> In the near future, the U.S. media and the Asian economy might well become the world's two greatest powers. Compared with that, "pluralist Europe," which is characterized by intellect, will perhaps be able to attain the position of third most powerful. As the third global power, the countries of Europe might be able to return to a state of full employment and to restrain and resolve conflicts around the world. In this respect, Europe should be viewed as pluralist rather

---

11. Jacques Attali, *Europamirai no Sentaku*, trans. Hisanori Isomura (Tokyo: Harashobō, 1995), pp. 207–08 (my translation).

than unified and, consequently, should strive to be a place where many peoples coexist rather than a place of imposed unification. The fact that many things exist in a single place is an important trump card for Europe.[12]

While zigzagging and backtracking along the path envisioned by Attali, the dream of union is being realized in Europe. The important point here is that, while achieving the goal of integration, the countries of Europe are also achieving gradual expansion of their markets and democratization of their systems. This structural reform was needed to bring about the third path. Much of European structural reform consisted of the introduction of competition through the market, which was a type of Americanization. In other words, Europe accepted and effectuated the Americanization of its economy for the cause of European unification and in order to become the counterbalance to the power of the United States. It never was, however, extreme Americanization or market expansion, because it was a policy for the purpose of maintaining the identities, histories, and cultures of the various countries and regions of pluralist Europe. They are, thus, creating a new unified Europe that is well suited to the new network globalization.[13]

About two years ago at a dinner party, I debated with Jean Lemierre, the President of the European Bank for Reconstruction and Development (EBRD), the reasons for Japan's inability to drastically reform a system which, though successful in the past, had begun to break down. In the course of that debate and the ensuing discussion of the policies Japan and Asia should implement to resolve the situation, Lemierre perceptively said: "Sakakibara, the answer is clear. Europe and France had a clear cause for structural reform. It was the unification of Europe. There is no cause for Japan. Without a cause, it is difficult to impose reforms that are going to be painful to many citizens."

Asian Regional Cooperation and Japanese Structural Reform

As if to follow European movement toward unification, the United States announced that by 2005 there would be an American free trade area

---

12. Ibid.

13. In a way, it is a grand experiment to attempt to resolve the contradiction pointed out by Rodrik between the market and democracy. To put it in Noda's terms, it may be the rebirth of a type of empire, rather than Attali's "third power," where Europe would be a counterbalance to U.S. power, potentially dividing the world into two camps.

comprising thirty-four countries. Since the establishment of a European empire, an American empire is now being built in the North and South American continents. Along these lines, even in Asia, which is far behind in regional integration, there is a mounting interest in regional cooperation. Although the Chiang Mai Initiative of May 2000 and ASEAN-plus-Three (Association of Southeast Asian Nations) are manifestations of this interest, the regional cooperation movement is still in the early stages.[14] The fundamental problems of how to handle relations with the United States and how to respond as a region to network globalization have not yet been fully resolved. It is not yet clear if Asian regional cooperation or regional union is going to become "the cause" for Japan and Asia as European unification was for Europe. In the case of Japan and other Asian countries, structural reform has not always resulted in internally driven change, even though it is perhaps the most important issue. In Thailand and South Korea, for instance, structural reform was, for the most part, imposed by the International Monetary Fund (IMF) and the United States, resulting in very strong opposition from the citizens of those countries. In Japan, structural reform is still just a vague concept. Much of it is only an expression of dissatisfaction against the old regime.

In Japan a sense of purpose and a vision of the future, rather than simple market expansion or Americanization, is an absolute necessity for internally motivated structural reform to take place. Just as European revival was Europe's dream following a long period of suffering, after ten or more years of enduring the "Japanese disease," Japan could begin to view revival as a goal. Yet, compared to Japan's goal of catching up with the developed world through modernization in the hundred years since the Meiji Restoration, revival seems too limited and short term as a goal. Even if European style unification were to be impossible for Japan and Asia, Japan still should pursue structural reform in order to maintain its prominent position in Asia and as the third major power in the world, after the United States and Europe.

Implementation of structural reform from within, however, has the serious tendency to stall because of competing vested interests. In order to endure the pain of reform, it is important for Japan to have a firm sense of identity as a nation and as a part of a region through culture and history.

---

14. The ASEAN member countries are Brunei Darussalam, Cambodia, Indonesia, Lao PDR, Malaysia, Myanmar, the Philippines, Singapore, Thailand, and Vietnam. The "plus-Three" countries are China, Japan, and South Korea.

Furthermore, structural reform that is externally imposed is likely to generate a backlash, such as anti-Americanism and anti-globalization.

The issue of Asian regional cooperation or unification is discussed later in this book, keeping in mind that internally motivated structural reform is a precondition. The next chapter reviews Japan's modern system since the Meiji Era, focusing specifically on structurally reforming Japanese-style capitalism, a process which was finally completed after World War II. This structural reform neither flatters capitalism nor Americanization. Once again, the intention of structural reform is to maintain, and develop in the context of the world's new environment of internationalism, the pluralism of Japan and the rest of Asia, including each country's cultural identity.

2 | Japan's Modernization and Industrialization

As in the case of other Asian countries, Japan's modernization was externally prompted. Although the first sign of this for the *bakufu* was the arrival of Commodore Perry and the Black Ships, the United States had turned its attention inward because of the Civil War.[1] It was England, therefore, that pressured Japan to modernize. The period from the Meiji Restoration to World War I was an age of globalization under *Pax Britannica*. After the institution-building period of the Meiji Restoration, Japan signed a treaty with England in 1902 and solidified its position in Asia.

In the nineteenth century, after engaging in the opium trade and the subsequent Opium War, England completely

---

1. During the Edo period, the government was called the *bakufu*. Commodore Perry is credited with opening up Japan to trade and commerce in 1854 by convincing the Japanese to sign the U.S.-Japan Treaty of Kanagawa. Japan had been virtually isolated since the 1600s with the exception that the Dutch were allowed limited entry into the port of Nagasaki. Perry's expeditionary force for the 1854 landing in Japan included eight ships, i.e., frigates (paddle wheel steamers), sloops (sailing vessels), and supply ships. The Japanese called these ships "Kurofune" (black ships) because of their dark color and the black

controlled China and forced the ideas of English capitalism and free trade on it and other countries of Asia. The result could be called a forced free trade system. It forced inward-looking Asia, including China (from the Ming Dynasty on), which had ceased its maritime expeditions, and Japan, which was isolated, to look outward again. Although Japan and Thailand avoided colonization, they were woven into the free trade system without power over their customs duties—under various peace treaties in the case of Japan, and under the Polling Treaty, in the case of Thailand. In this way, trade, which had become regional and limited from the late seventeenth to the eighteenth century, became globalized again under English hegemony. Moreover, the English capitalist system took root, albeit tentatively, in Asia and in Japan.

Describing the Japanese economy from the Taisho to the Meiji period, Takafusa Nakamura states that "society at that time still had old fashioned . . . nineteenth century ideas, such as capitalism, that had survived around the world from the time of Marx and Engels."[2] Classical capitalist colonial operations also existed in the rest of Asia. The plantation economies of Burma, Thailand, the Malay Peninsula, Sumatra, and the Philippines were examples of this. Yonosuke Hara writes the same thing about Southeast Asian plantation agriculture. "The structural principle behind the economy had individualism and competition as its base and was completely different from the obligations of the ruler and the subject under absolutist rule," he says. "The capitalist principles could be said to have functioned purely on their own."[3]

Japan's Difference

The only difference between Japan and colonized Asia was that Japan, by the Edo period, had achieved a certain level of modernization and had completed the agricultural revolution, which Akira Hayami calls the "industrious" revolution.[4] During the Edo period, the government's monopolistic trade system of *sakoku*, or national isolation, which shaped

---

smoke spewed by the coal-burning steamships. In addition, the ships appeared threatening because they carried a total of over a hundred of the latest naval cannons.

2. Takafusa Nakamura, *Shōwa Kēzaishi*, Iwanami Seminar Book 17 (Tokyo: Iwanami Books, 1986), p. 7 (my translation).

3. Yonosuke Hara, *Ajia Dainamizumu* (Tokyo: NTT Shuppansha, 1996), pp. 56–57 (my translation).

4. Akira Hayami, Osamu Saito, and Shinya Sugiyama, eds., *Tokugawa Shakai kara no Tembō* (Tokyo: Dōbunkan Shuppan, 1989).

modern Japanese society during a nascent period, constituted a complete social and economic system.[5] Although that changed during the Meiji period under the English-led free trade system, the "industrious" revolution of the Edo period should not be forgotten. Or, to put it another way, the modern Japanese system was already complete in its own way, having previously experienced a religious revolution and a renaissance during the Kamakura and Muromachi periods.[6]

If one objectively analyzes the Edo period under the 260 years of Tokugawa rule, Japanese civilization was rich and full of vitality and creativity, although Marxists and others who focused on the plight of poor farmers and on the farmer riots may not have shared the same assessment.

According to Tsuneo Sato, the agricultural structure of the Edo period was quite varied. The region of Koshu, at the end of the Edo period, for example, had industries of silk, cotton, and rice.[7] Furthermore, the level of productivity was particularly high. From the mid-Edo period to 1881, it was approximately the same as that from 1881 to the Showa period. The farmers raised silkworms, cotton, sugar cane, and many other products. Furthermore, the idea of a goods-based economy had begun to take hold.

Even the much-studied farmer riots only amounted to one outbreak every one hundred years, if they are divided among the several hundred thousand towns in the country. According to Sato, with the exception of unusual circumstances such as natural disasters and starvation, the structure could be characterized as having an element of group bargaining with regard to taxation of farmers. The lords of the domains would not intrude in the affairs of the village, and the self-governance of farmers was virtually complete.[8] Although it was claimed by earlier historians that 50 to 60 percent of production went to pay taxes, it is now estimated that the real level of taxation was only 10 to 20 percent.[9]

In addition to wealthy farm villages, the Edo period was notable for its vibrant city culture with distinctive regional flavors. During that time, Edo

5. *Sakoku* was the policy of national isolation under the Edo government, which completely closed Japan to the rest of the world with the exception of China and Holland, which were allowed to trade only in government sanctioned ports.

6. The Kamakura (1185–1333) and Muromachi (1338–1573) periods preceded the Edo (1600–1867) and Meiji (1868–1912) periods.

7. Tsuneo Satō and Shinzaburō Oishi, *Hinnōshikan o Minaosu* (Tokyo: Kōdansha Jidaishinsho, 1995).

8. The agricultural villages of the Edo period had established self-governance based on three functional groups (that is, village heads, group leaders, and farmers' representatives).

9. Satō and Oishi, *Hinnōshikan o Minaosu*, p. 116.

itself was one of the few cities in the world that had a population close to one million inhabitants. In addition to Edo and the commercial capital, Osaka, and the cultural capital, Kyoto, cities had sprung up around castles all over the country, and these were connected by a regularly maintained system of roads.

The Meiji Restoration was a major transformation that brought Japan into the world system. The previously created system of the Edo period, however, had actually been perpetuated. Eiichi Yazawa states that the Meiji Restoration had changed the "structure at the top of the *bakuhan* system," while "the base had hardly changed."[10]

According to Chie Nakane, it was the autonomous villages and samurai as bureaucrats without land ownership that came to fundamentally characterize the Edo period.[11] According to this model, the village communities were maintained as they were after the Meiji Restoration, while samurai, who lost their elite status as the ruling class, maintained their function as bureaucrats or salaried workers. Government policies were generally centralized after the Meiji Restoration under the Meiji Constitution, but there was also quite a bit of decentralization in regional policy with regard to the cities, towns, and villages, where Edo characteristics were, to a significant degree, retained. For example, from the beginning, the cities, towns, and villages had the power to establish their own rules and regulations, and even mayors, although not publicly elected, were selected after being nominated by a village congress. Country squires and influential people of the village were chosen to be on these nominating congresses. The structure of the village with the landowners at the center was further strengthened during the Meiji period because many small farmers became sharecroppers under a new policy that required people to pay their land tax with money rather than with rice and other agricultural products.

While continuing to maintain the somewhat modern village system that had developed during the Edo period, the Meiji government needed fundamental social structure reform in order to strengthen the sense of national unity and identity necessary for survival in the competitive global environment. The first reform measures were instituted in 1872 when *han*

10. Shinzaburō Ōishi and Chie Nakane (eds.), *Edo Jidai to Kindaika* (Tokyo: Chikuma Shobō, 1986), p. 462 (my translation). The *bakuhan* system was the system of governance during the Edo period, by which the government (*bakufu*) administered the country and the domains (*han*) sustained the government.

11. Chie Nakane, "Edo Jidai no Ninaite Toshiteno Shakaikaisō," in Ōishi and Nakane, *Edo Jidai to Kindaika.*

(feudal domains) were changed to prefectures, effectively bringing them under the control of the central government by having the governors appointed by the central government.

The second group of measures included the abolition of official social hierarchy, the establishment of new education policy, and the establishment of a meritocracy. One of the important legacies of the Meiji Restoration was the spread to the masses of the ideology of meritocracy and self-made success. The Meiji leaders, who themselves had suffered under the kinship system of the Edo period and were convinced of its detrimental effect on society, abolished the system. Joseph Alexander von Hübner, a leading Austrian diplomat at the time who was at the conference on August 3, 1872, between Takayoshi Kido and the British Counsel, was very impressed by Kido's conviction. He recalls Kido saying that, "three years is enough time to completely get rid of the right of heredity and change the citizens' practice and thinking."[12] Around this time, Yukichi Fukuzawa, the noted education pioneer of the time, coined the phrase "lineage is the enemy of the parent," by which he meant that people's lives should not be decided by their birth and that success should result from the effort of the individual.[13]

Prosperous Nation, Strong Military— Japan's Industrial Revolution

Ryōtarō Shiba was precisely on target when he chose to portray the Meiji nation by focusing on the Russo-Japanese War and the Battle of the Sea of Japan and tell the story through the brothers Yoshifuru and Saneyuki Akiyama in his book *Saka no Ue no Kumo,* which translates as "Clouds over the Hill."[14] The most important tasks for Japan at that time were to have a modern military, to adapt to the free trade system that was forced upon it, and to pursue seriously the opening of the country. In view of this, the Battle of the Sea of Japan was a symbolic event. After more than two hundred years of isolation, Japan as a seafaring and trading nation found it nec-

12. Joseph Alexander von Hübner, *Osutoria Gaikokan no Meiji Ishin,* trans. Shinichi Ichikawa and Masahiro Matsumoto (Tokyo: Shin Jimbutsu Orai-sha, 1988), p. 7 (my translation). Original: M. le Baron de Hübner, *Promenade autour du Monde 1871* (Paris: Hachette, 1877).

13. Yukichi Fukuzawa, *Fukuo Jiden* (Tokyo: Keio Tsushin-sha, 1994), p. 9 (my translation).

14. Ryōtarō Shiba, *Saka no Ue no Kumo,* vols. I–VI (Tokyo: Bungeishunju, 1969–72).

essary to carve out a position for itself in the world. The Battle of the Sea of Japan could be regarded as the equivalent of the 1571 Battle of Lepanto for Venice and England's 1588 victory over the Spanish Armada.

In parallel with the military victories of the Russo-Japanese War and the Sino-Japanese War, Japan's textile industry strengthened its position in Asia. For Japan, this was the equivalent of England's Industrial Revolution a century earlier. Heita Kawakatsu sees Japan's Industrial Revolution as part of Asia's reorganization of the regional cotton industry rather than as the forced total reorganization of Japan's domestic industries after the country's opening to the world:

> India was the first to import British textile machinery. India, which had the East Asian domestic textile market (both the short and long thread market), expanded its exports in the 1860s and 1870s and became very involved in East Asia's supply of and demand for cotton. The development of Japan's textile industry was intended to prevent India's economic encroachment. From the point of view of Japan's textile industry, Japan's industrial revolution can be generally seen as the process by which Japan came to hold a dominant position in what was the manifestation of the subconscious conflicts within Asia, rather than as the natural extension of the European industrial revolution that had begun in England.[15]

In this way, the Meiji nation, while looking up at the "the clouds above the hill," built a prosperous nation and a strong military and solidified its position in the global, modern capitalist system. It was an effort to survive within the rules of "forced free trade" in the global economy under English hegemony as well as to secure its position as a modern military and capitalist nation, while at the same time continuing the modern legacy of the Edo period. This process was also a part of the goal of "Out of Asia and into Europe," a phrase coined by Yukichi Fukuzawa.[16] Modernization was accompanied by Europeanization. Although this could not be helped in light of Europe's military and industrial dominance, as pointed out by

15. Heita Kawakatsu, *Nihon Bunmē to Kindai Sēyō—Sakoku Saikō,* NHK Book 627 (Tokyo: Nihon Hōsō Shuppan Kyōkai, 1991), p. 89 (my translation).
16. Fukuzawa, *Fukuo Jiden,* p. 9 (my translation).

Kyōji Watanabe, what was good about a very special period in history, the Edo period, has been lost due to modernization.[17]

From Two World Wars to Japanese Style Capitalism

World War I, pitting the United Kingdom and France against Germany, eventually involved the United States, and thus became a great battle that brought the end of British-led globalization. It was the end of *Pax Britannica* and free trade, or rather forced free trade. Particularly in Asia, it became a period of new nationalism and new nation states. Although at the beginning of the twentieth century, much of Asia was still under colonial control, the end of the free trade system had great consequences for colonial management. For example, India was given the right to determine its own customs duties and then pursued import-substitution industrialization. In East Asia, national bureaucracies protected and nurtured industry and intervened in economic management in order to protect colonial economies. After World War II, these movements gradually became the economic framework supporting the new nation-state system that would emerge from political independence.

What should be stressed here is that this movement was not limited to Japan but was part of a larger historical movement. With the end of *Pax Britannica* and the collapse of classical capitalism, the world's nations began to look inward for a new national design.

The economic frameworks of the various countries that were formed between World Wars I and II continued until the 1970s, albeit with a few modifications. Japan, although it experienced some changes after the end of the high-growth period, has only recently, in the twenty-first century, begun its large-scale regime transformation and structural reform.

The Final Phase of the Development of Japanese Capitalism

In 1955, the year the foundation was being laid for the high growth period to come, Japan's total population was less than 90 million and total employment was over 40 million. Those engaged in the primary sector, mainly agriculture, were still 15 million strong, far more than those engaged in the secondary sector of manufacturing, which were less than 10 million. The tertiary sector (that is, the wholesale, retail, and service

17. Kyōji Watanabe, *Yukishi Yo No Omokage* (Tokyo: Ashi Shobō, 1998).

industries) included mainly those who were self-employed and their families. Japan at that time was still very much an agricultural society. The landscape of farming villages (in other words, the structure of agriculture) had
not changed fundamentally since the beginning of the Meiji era. The rice
paddies around the farm villages, the cows and horses, and the cultivation
methods using plows and sickles had remained relatively unchanged. At the
time of the Meiji Restoration, those in the agriculture sector numbered
about 15 million, not very different from the number at the beginning of
the high growth period (1955–70). Although manufacturing shifted from
textiles to iron ore and heavy industry, the newly created jobs were filled by
an increasing number of workers entering the labor market for the first
time, which meant that the highly autonomous villages were basically pre-
served as they were in the Edo period.

The postwar period of high growth brought about significant structural
change in the villages, the completion of Japan's modernization and industrialization, and the establishment of the Japanese capitalist system. In
1960, Osamu Shimomura, who as an adviser to Prime Minister Hayato
Ikeda had pushed high growth policies, praised the potential of Japan's
economy in the following manner:

> The Japanese economy is now at a historical threshold. The freeing
> of people's creativity is the force behind this unprecedented enthusi-
> asm. In spite of the economic growth rate of 17 percent in [1959],
> which was a sudden economic expansion, the fact that the economy
> is extremely stable is proof of the Japanese economy's strength. The
> will and the ability of private sector businessmen, managers, engi-
> neers, and workers to modernize and increase productivity have
> already yielded these results. As long as the nurturing of this ability is
> not neglected, it will be possible for the Japanese economy to con-
> tinue its rapid growth. We believe that in the next few decades, there
> is the possibility of increasing the GNP by 2.5 to 3 times rather than
> just 2 times. This type of rapid growth will create revolutionary
> change in all economic activity.[18]

Much research has been done on Japan's high growth period. Without
reviewing it thoroughly here, the main point is that during this period

---

18. Osamu Shimomura, "Sēchōsēsaku no Kihonmondai," *Kinyūzasējijō*, vol. 518 (1960), p. 20 (my
translation).

Japanese capitalism, which emerged in the 1930s and developed through postwar reforms, flourished. Although it was very different than the classical capitalism developed under the forced free trade system of the Taisho period and early Showa period, the new system was consistent with the nation-state-centered capitalist system of the world.

The force behind this high growth was the private sector. The *zaibatsu* were abolished, ownership and management were separated, and the foundation was laid for young professional managers to aggressively pursue new corporate goals. Through an economic purge, many business leaders left their positions, and young managers, who were mid-level salaried workers in their forties, came to power and tended to follow an aggressive management style. As the old order collapsed, the Anti-Trust Law and the Anti-Monopoly Law were enacted as competition had become fierce and an aggressive management style the norm.

As a result of the loss of the war and the abolition of the *zaibatsu*, investors took a beating and the direct capital market stopped functioning. Consequently, an indirect financing system centered on banks and tightly regulated by authorities was formed. It is in the context of such factors as direct loans from the Bank of Japan, the issuance of large bank debentures by long-term trust banks, and the massive concentration of bank deposits that Japanese financial institutions responded to the immense demand for capital during the high growth period.

Capital accumulation alone cannot, however, sustain growth over the long term. Technology and other factors also play a role. Although foreign technology was imported to fill the vacuum created by the war, Japan itself had stored up technology before and during the war, and the progressive corporate groups of the prewar period (that is, Toyota, Hitachi, and Riken Kagaku) became one of the pillars supporting high growth. Nakamura, for example, describes this process as follows:

> It cannot be denied that behind post-war heavy industry, there were not only many heavy industrial facilities that were being built for the military, but there was also the nurturing of engineers and workers who had learned the technology in the factories. As factories that produced machine guns during the war switched to making sewing machines and those making optic weapons switched to cameras and eyeglasses, what was accumulated in the facilities—technology and labor—had a large influence on the later direction of the Japanese economy. It was also during the war that the system of subcontract-

ing spread, solidifying after the war. Although, at first, the large corporations involved with munitions took the position that they would produce the parts in-house, eventually they created a system of subcontracting out parts and other things to small and mid-size companies. Although it was an emergency measure to increase production, at the same time, it was an opportunity to improve the technology of small and mid-size companies and the standard of production. For the small and mid-size firms that were affiliated with the heavy industries, to secure orders and develop was decisive. This is the origin of the long-lasting relationship between the small and mid-size companies and their parent companies.[19]

In this way, the large exporting corporations that were the engines for high growth absorbed the pre-war Japanese and foreign technology to create a network that was to be called the *keiretsu,* where mid-level small- and mid-sized companies came under the leadership of dynamic professional managers in the larger corporations.

On the other hand, the public sector supported farm villages, which were facing large structural changes, by controlling the price of rice and wheat. At the same time, it supported construction of necessary infrastructure by aggressively promoting public works. While the outflow of labor from the farm villages filled manufacturing jobs, it was also absorbed into industries, such as construction, which had expanded due to rapid growth of public works. From 1955 to 1970, employment in the agriculture and forestry industries declined from 14.75 million to 8.42 million, while manufacturing rose from 7.57 million to 13.77 million. In the construction industry the increase was from 1.95 million to 3.94 million. At the time, the newly constructed infrastructure, including roads, ports, and high-speed rail lines, had very high marginal productivity and brought large external economic dividends to the private manufacturing industry. Through fiscal investment and loan programs, public funds such as postal savings and pensions were directed to entities like the Japan Development Bank, the Japan Highway Public Corporation, and the Electric Power Development Company to support growth from the periphery. While the value of public financing, public corporations, and public enterprises is being questioned now, they served a purpose during the high growth period.

---

19. Takafusa Nakamura, *Nihon Kēzai—sono Sēchou to Kōzō* (Tokyo: Tokyo Daigaku Shuppansha, 1978), p. 136 (my translation).

High growth enabled the Japanese economy to catch up to those of Europe and the United States. What was remarkable about the last structural reform under Japanese modernization was that it happened without large-scale political or social upheaval. That was the Japanese miracle. It was also what European and U.S. Japanologists called "Japan Inc.," which was underpinned by the highly efficient, cooperative relationship between the public and private sectors. Although private manufacturing was the engine for growth (and, in that sense, the growth was driven by competition in the market), the public sector also played an important part in the process by building public infrastructure and providing social stability.

3 | Formation and Collapse of the Public Construction State

To appreciate the complexities of the modern Japanese state, one must understand that Japanese civilization went through a period of creative destruction before it became a public construction state. Initially, Japan was a largely agricultural state characterized by lush vegetation. Almost without exception, the beauty of the country and how the Japanese cherished it impressed those who visited Japan from the end of the Edo period through the early Meiji period.

The Garden or Agricultural State

Sir Rutherford Alcock stated that "such fertility of soil, fine growth of ornamental timber, richness and variety of foliage, or such perfection of care and neatness in the hedge rows and shady lanes, the gardens, and the numerous pleasure grounds of the temples, are not, I believe, to be found anywhere [else] out of England."[1]

1. Sir Rutherford Alcock, K.C.B., *The Capital of the Tycoon: A Narrative of a Three Years' Residence in Japan,* vol. 1, reprint (St. Clair Shores, Mich.: Scholarly

Robert Fortune felt the same way:

> A remarkable feature in the Japanese character is that even . . . the lowest classes . . . have an inherent love for flowers, and find in the cultivation of a few pet plants an endless source of recreation and unalloyed pleasure. If this be one of the tests of a high state of civilization amongst a people, the lower orders amongst the Japanese come out in a most favorable light when contrasted with the same classes amongst [the English]."[2]

To the two men, the harmonious people of Japan seemed truly fortunate to live in a country that appeared to be a garden state, possibly even more than England. This idyllic civilization had been peaceful and wealthy for 265 years during the Edo period and had experienced remarkable productivity growth via the "industrious" revolution by the end of the nineteenth century.[3]

Kyōji Watanabe claimed that this civilization was destroyed by modernization. Describing the inevitable end of the Edo civilization that he believed occurred by the end of Meiji, he writes:

> It should clearly be stated that no matter how the drama of contemporary Japan might be described, it could not have started without the strangulation and death of a civilization. All would agree that the strangulation and death were necessary and even constituted progress. If we do not ask what it was that perished or was destroyed, we will not be able to comprehend its nature, let alone figure out the significance of the drama.[4]

Press, 1968 [1863]), p. 201. Sir Rutherford Alcock (1809–97) was a diplomat and was appointed Britain's first consul-general in Japan in 1858. He is known for bringing Japanese art to Europe and for writing this book about his three-year experience in Japan.

2. Robert Fortune, *Yedo and Peking: A Narrative of a Journey to the Capitals of Japan and China* (London: John Murray, 1863), pp. 92–93. Robert Fortune (1812–80) traveled to China, Japan, and other Asian countries to collect plants. He was responsible for the introduction of 120 species of plants to the West and was instrumental in establishing the tea industry in India.

3. "Industrious revolution" as used here refers to the term coined by Akira Hayami, who describes the agricultural revolution in Japan during the Tokugawa (Edo) period as different from an industrial revolution in that production was increased through an increase in the investment of labor rather than in the investment of capital. (See chapter 2.)

4. Kyōji Watanabe, *Yukishi Yo No Omokage* (Tokyo: Ashi Shobō, 1998), pp. 7–8 (my translation). Watanabe is a lecturer at the Kawai Juku in Fukuoka, Japan.

Development of the Public Works Regime since the Meiji Period

From around 1880, when the conflict and confusion of the Restoration abated, the Meiji government aggressively pursued infrastructure investment in public works with the goal of remodeling Japan. The government achieved this by creating fixed capital for flood control, the railroad, roads, ports, fisheries, forestry, and telephone and telegraph infrastructure. At the beginning of the 1880s there was considerable investment in water works, but by the end of the 1880s this had shifted to the railroad.

During the forty years between the second decade of the Meiji period and the beginning of the Showa period, 40 to 50 percent of infrastructure investment was directed to the railroad. The railroad was the most important investment recipient during the Meiji and Taisho periods for economic, political, and military reasons (although its importance was partially due to the fact that there was no other industry that required large sums of concentrated investment). Investment ensured that Japan would have a wide-reaching railroad infrastructure that unified the country as a modern military nation.

Until the National Railroad Law was enacted in 1906, private railroads had a better network than the public railroad. After the creation of the national railroad, the situation reversed: By 1907 the national railroad network covered 7,166 kilometers, almost ten times that of the private railroads. The push for the creation of a national railroad and railroad investment came from the Seiyūkai political party and Kei Hara, who, along with Kakuei Tanaka, was a proponent of local benefits.[5]

Taichirō Mitani stated that Kei Hara's "railroad politics" were "the most important part of Taisho democracy and led to the process of party politics. The shift in provincial benefits from the 'land tax politics' phase to the 'railroad politics' phase was one of the important characteristics of Taisho democracy."[6] Tetsuo Najita stated that while Kei Hara "increased taxes, issued internal and external bonds, built more schools, roads, dams, and railroads than ever before and tried to stimulate the economy. The goal of dispersing public funds was to expand the power of the party and link the

5. The Seiyūkai was founded in 1900 and remained the most powerful party in Japan until 1921. Kei Hara (1856–1921) was an influential politician in the early twentieth century and was a cofounder of the Rikken Seiyūkai Party. He served as the first "commoner" prime minister in Japan (1918–1921). For Tanaka, see note 11, below.

6. Taichirō Mitani, *Nihon Sētōseji no Kēsē* (Tokyo: Tokyo Daigaku Shuppankai, 1967), p. 21 (my translation). Mitani is a professor of political science at Seikei University in Tokyo.

activities at party headquarters with that of the provincial, prefectural, and local levels." Although "going through the bureaucracy to fulfill the economic demands of the provinces is nothing new . . . before, it was almost purely a provincial matter; now, at the end of Meiji, it is built into national policy by politicians."[7]

In this analysis one could substitute Kakuei Tanaka for Kei Hara, change the time period, and the analysis would essentially still fit. The construction state system that Tanaka completed was implemented before the war by Toru Hoshi, Kei Hara, Korekiyo Takahashi, and by the political parties Seiyūkai and Minseito.[8]

From the latter half of the 1910s, the amount of investment in roads grew and roads replaced the railroad as the recipient of the largest portion of infrastructure investment. By 1930, the size of the shares of investment in the railroad and roads reversed. Particularly under Finance Minister Takahashi's Emergency Rescue Plan (1932 to 1934), which was drawn up in response to the Showa Depression, roads, fisheries, and forestry received the bulk of investment.[9] In the first year of the plan, road investment was 41 percent of total public works expenditure and fisheries and forestry accounted for 12 percent. This Emergency Rescue Plan, which was carried out through the combined efforts of Hara and Takahashi, was a very Keynesian, farm village rescue-type policy that created the pattern for later public works–centered finance policy. It also became the foundation for the completion of the construction state and the remodeling of Japan under Kakuei Tanaka.

It is possible that Tanaka's success in developing a construction state marked the end point of the modernization and industrialization that had been occurring since the Meiji Restoration. Having been exposed to Western colonialism, the garden state had to be remade into an efficient industrialized nation to successfully fight a major war. Japan's modernization and industrialization was pursued even as farm villages were maintained as self-governing entities, as they had been since the Meiji period.

Table 3-1 shows the percentage of GDP the government spent on infrastructure investment during the prewar and postwar periods. During the

7. Tetsuo Najita, *Hara Kei—Sējigijyutsu no Kyoshō,* trans. Shiro Yasuda (Tokyo: Yomiuri Shimbunsha, 1974), pp. 104, 106 (my translation). Najita is Robert S. Ingersoll Distinguished Service Professor of History and of East Asian Languages and Civilizations at the University of Chicago.

8. The Minseitō existed from 1927 to 1940 as one of the major political parties of the Showa period.

9. The Showa Depression was part of the global depression that followed the stock market crash of 1929.

Table 3-1. *Japanese Infrastructure Investment*

Period	Percent of GDP	Period	Percent of GDP
1877–1901	2.7	1948–63	4.6
1902–06	2.6	1964–74	4.8
1907–12	2.8	1975–80	5.6
1913–17	2.3	1981–90	5.3
1918–34	3.2	1991–96	6.0
1935–40	2.6		

Source: Data for 1877–1963 are from Moriyuki Sawamoto, *Kōkyōtōshi Hyakunen no Ayumi—Nihon no Kēzai to Tomoni* (Tokyo: Ōseishuppansha, 1981), p. 73. Data for 1964–96 are from *OECD National Accounts*, vol. 2 (1981, 1989, 1998).

prewar period, from the beginning of the Hara Government in 1918 to the Emergency Rescue Plan under Hara and Takahashi, this figure was the highest at 3.2 percent. Infrastructure investment increased in the postwar period, and reached 6 percent between 1990 and 1996 after the completion of the construction state. The basic structure of public investment was actually created between 1910 and 1935 under the leadership of Hara and the Seiyūkai and then continued through the prewar and postwar periods.

In general, the allocation of public works funds did not vary greatly between 1935 and 1965. The national railroad share stayed at the same level and the road construction share stayed in the thirtieth percentile, as illustrated in table 3-2. The stability in the sector share of all public works expenditures between 1980 and 2000 can be seen in table 3-3. In particular, road

Table 3-2. *Breakdown of Public Works–Related Expenditures*
Percent

Sector	1935	1965
Rivers	16.1	12.4
National railroad	18.7	18.6
Roads	38.3	30.4
Ports	7.6	4.8
Agriculture and fisheries	9.3	12.7
Forestry conservation	1.6	1.6
Telephone and telegraph	8.4	19.6

Source: Compiled from Sawamoto, *Kōkyōtōshi Hyakunen no Ayumi*, pp. 282–83.

Table 3-3. *Change in Public Works–Related Expenditures*

Percent

Type of works	1980	1982	1984	1986	1988	1990	1992	1994	1996	1998	2000
Forestry and water conservation	17.38	17.38	17.40	17.53	17.60	17.66	17.80	17.88	17.03	15.69	15.94
Road construction and maintenance	30.07	29.72	29.66	29.13	28.97	29.08	28.78	28.04	28.12	30.10	29.67
Harbor and airport construction and maintenance	8.31	8.22	8.23	8.25	8.26	8.37	8.11	7.77	7.59	7.62	7.75
Residential area	11.87	12.07	12.14	12.33	12.48	12.43	11.70	11.44	12.74	11.98	12.63
Sewer, environmental, sanitation facility construction and maintenance	15.21	15.50	15.53	15.71	15.66	15.57	16.84	17.81	17.91	18.26	17.97
Agriculture and farm-village construction and maintenance	14.21	14.12	14.13	14.15	14.15	14.15	13.87	13.45	12.86	12.15	11.68
Forest preservation: main road construction and maintenance	2.84	2.80	2.74	2.72	2.71	2.57	2.75	3.48	3.59	3.81	3.96
Unspecified	0.21	0.18	0.17	0.17	0.17	0.17	0.16	0.13	0.16	0.38	0.41

Source: Compiled from Japan, Ministry of Finance, *Zaisei Tōkei* (2000).

construction and maintenance expenditures, which are backed by a special fund, were almost unchanged at around 30 percent.

The Final Transition to the Construction State

Kyōji Watanabe claimed that "culture cannot be destroyed, and neither can some ethnic characteristics; they can only be transformed. What can be destroyed is civilization—life as a whole, as a historical entity."[10] If the modernization of Japan was ultimately achieved through post-war high growth, then the high-growth period was the end of the civilization characterized by the garden state. What emerged from the destruction of one civilization was the rise of another, the public construction state. This was characterized by a shift in employment from agriculture to construction.

During the high-growth period, agricultural employment rapidly declined, while employment in the construction industry dramatically increased, from 1.95 million in 1955 to 4.79 million in 1975. When Kakuei Tanaka became prime minister in 1972,[11] employment in the construction industry surpassed employment in the agricultural industry: male employment in agriculture declined from 3.66 million in 1971 to 3.39 million in 1972, while male employment in construction rose from 3.60 million in 1971 to 3.77 million in 1972. By 2000, agricultural employment was 2.97 million, while construction employment was 6.53 million, more than double that of agriculture.

Part of the reason for this dramatic increase in construction employment was the passage of legislation favorable to the construction industry. Tanaka successfully pushed for the passage of a permanent special fund for gasoline in 1958, along with three new laws: the New Road Law in 1952, the Temporary Rented Land Law in 1953, and the Emergency Road Maintenance Rented Land Law in 1958. As table 3-4 illustrates, the later levy of national and local taxes, such as the Liquefied Petroleum Gas Tax, the Motor Vehicle Tonnage Tax, and the Local Road Tax provided substantial financial resources for the construction of public roads. In pushing for parliamentary legislation enacted by his own initiative and not through the

10. Watanabe, *Yukishi Yo No Omokage*, p. 7 (my translation).

11. Kakuei Tanaka (1918–93) was a political leader of Japan. He was a member of the Liberal Democratic Party who served in a number of government posts, including minister of finance and minister of international trade and industry. He was also prime minister from 1972 until 1974, when he was forced to resign.

Table 3-4. *Special Road Resources*[a]

Tax item (year established)	Tax rate	Proportion for roads	2001 Tax revenue, yen
National			
Gasoline Tax (1949); special fund since 1954	Temporary: 48.6/liter; principal: 24.3/liter[b]	Total revenue[c]	2.84 trillion
Liquified Petroleum Gas (LPG) Tax (1966)	Principal: 17.5/kg	50% of revenue (other 50% transferred to local as LPG Transfer Tax)	14 billion
Motor Vehicle Tonnage (MVT) Tax (1971)	Temporary: 6,300/0.5 ton year; principal: 2,500/0.5 ton year[d]	80% of national's 75%[e]	675.3 billion
Total national			3.53 trillion[f]
Local			
Local Road Tax (1955)	Temporary: 5.2/liter; principal: 4.4/liter	Total revenue: 43% prefectures, 57% municipalities[g]	299 billion

LPG Transfer Tax (1966)	Principal: 17.5/kg	50% of national LPG Tax revenue	14.2 billion
MVT Transfer Tax (1971)	Temporary: 6,300/0.5 ton year; principal: 2,500/0.5 ton year	25% of national MVT Tax revenue	282.9 billion
Light Oil Delivery Tax (1956)	Temporary: 32.1/liter; principal: 15/liter	Total revenue to prefectures	1.25 trillion
Automobile Acquisition Tax (1968)	3% of price/value; 5% for noncommercial vehicles, 1974–2003	Total revenue: 30% prefectures, 70% municipalities	485.7 billion
Total local			2.33 trillion
Total			5.86 trillion

Source: Compiled from Japan, Ministry of Finance, Tax Bureau, "An Outline of Japanese Taxes, 2001–2002."

a. Tax revenue is from 2001 Early Budget and 2001 Local Finance Plan.

b. The temporary tax rate applies until the end of March 2003; for the MVT Tax, it applies until the end of April 2003.

c. From 1985, 1/15 went into a road maintenance special account. From 1988 to 2003, this was increased to 1/4.

d. Example.

e. Seventy-five percent of revenue is credited to the General Accounts of the State, with 80 percent of that for road resources.

f. In some cases, figures do not sum exactly.

g. "Prefectures" refers to all prefectures plus the twelve largest cities. "Municipalities refers to other cities, towns, and villages.

involvement of the administration, Tanaka was able to secure new resources and ensure favorable budget allocation for construction.

Tanaka's secretary at the time noted that Tanaka understood well the right of parliamentarians to propose and pass legislation. "Within a very short time, Tanaka was able to grasp the importance of the Diet's right to pass legislation under the new constitution and the system under which laws were enacted according to the will of parliamentarians. He would look back on that time and say that 'it has become a world where even one from a construction background can make laws if he becomes a parliamentarian.'"[12]

Tanaka utilized his power to ensure that the tax revenue was earmarked for special funds and that special accounts were created for public works. In addition to separating the management of the funds from that of the general account, which allowed for the expansion of public works expenditure, Tanaka employed public investment and loan programs to further his endeavors. From 1952 to 1959, eighteen new special accounts were created; of these, the main accounts were the Road Construction and Improvement Account (1958), the Special Multipurpose Dam Construction Account (1957), the National Land Improvement Account (1957), and the Special Port Facility Construction Account (1959). Table 3-5 shows that subsequently, there was a rapid increase in the budgets of public works–related special accounts. In particular, the Road Construction and Improvement Special Account increased twenty-fold over twenty years from FY1960 to FY1980 and reached ¥4,476.3 billion by FY2001. In 1955, funds used for constructing and improving roads accounted for 17 percent of public works; this rose to 32.2 percent in 1960 and increased to 45 percent by 1964.

Since 1955 the Trust Fund Bureau, which derives its resources from systems such as postal savings and public pension, has channeled large amounts of funds into public works through the creation of new public corporations. As table 3-6 shows, the Urban Development Corporation (formerly Housing and Urban Development Corporation) was founded in 1955 and the Japan Highway Public Corporation was founded in 1956; the establishment of public corporations such as the Metropolitan Expressway Public Corporation, the Hanshin Expressway Public Corporation, the Japan Railway Construction Public Corporation, and the Water Resources Development Public Corporation followed this. In addition, new public

---

12. Shigezō Hayasaka, *Seijika Tanaka Kakuei* (Tokyo: Chuōkōronsha, 1987), p. 15 (my translation).

Table 3-5. *Changes in Public Works–Related Special Accounts*
Billions of yen

Type of special account (year established)	1960	1970	1980	1990	2000	2001
Road construction and improvement (1958)	108.9	659.8	2,164.6	3,354.0	4,378.4	4,476.3
National schools (1964)	n.a.	305.4	1,295.9	1,988.8	2,702.8	2,742.8
Flood control (1960)	46.0	204.6	905.3	1,193.9	1,327.9	1,291.0
Special multipurpose dam construction (1957)	14.9	24.0	183.6	257.4	266.4	257.0
National land improvement (1957)	14.0	38.5	147.8	471.5	568.4	550.6
Harbor improvement (1961)	n.a.	93.5	310.9	402.7	453.7	444.2
Special port facility construction (1959)	9.5	14.3	6.1	8.9	16.6	14.6
Airport improvement (1970)	n.a.	18.5	219.1	378.8	494.1	484.1
National forest service (1947)	56.1	163.4	438.8	583.1	256.3	276.0
Forest conservation (1960)	6.1	31.2	152.4	174.8	192.3	188.1

Source: Compiled from Japan, Ministry of Finance, *Tokubetsu Kaikei Yosan* (annual).

corporations that were beneficiaries of public investment and loan programs, such as the Coal Producing Regional Development Corporation and the Coal Efficiency Corporation, were also formed at this time.

Thus the public works system of the construction state was formed via the establishment of special accounts, special funds, public corporations, and the general account through which construction bonds can be issued. Although the Japanese economy has experienced many changes, from high growth to stable growth and from the formation of a bubble to its collapse, the basic foundation of the construction state has not significantly changed, despite having undergone some modifications. The public works–centered finance structure is one of the fundamental pillars of the Japanese political-economic system, the modernization of which began before World War II and ended during the high-growth period.

Table 3-7 shows that the ratio of public works to GDP was still high even at the end of the twentieth century. For example, in 1997 the general government gross fixed capital formation was 5.7 percent of GDP in Japan,

Table 3-6. *Public Works–Related Public Corporations*

Title	Date established	Scale (millions of yen)[a]	Sample main projects
Teitō Rapid Transit Authority[b]	March 1941	467,805	Management of high-speed underground transit in Tokyo area
Urban Development Corporation[b]	July 1955	3,062,951	City area maintenance improvement, supplying rental housing and management
Japan Highway Public Corporation	April 1956	5,418,137	New construction, rebuilding, management of toll roads
Japan Green Resources Corporation[b]	July 1956	152,729	Maintenance of agricultural land and irrigation facilities, building of forest roads
Corporation for Advanced Transport and Technology	June 1959	128,098	Transfer of grants needed for railroad construction
Metropolitan Expressway Public Corporation	June 1959	850,980	Building, management of city highways in metropolitan areas
Hanshin Expressway Public Corporation	May 1962	646,563	Building, management of toll roads around Osaka, Kobe, and Kyoto
Water Resources Development Public Corporation	May 1962	365,688	Building, operating of dams and waterways
Japan Railway Construction Public Corporation	March 1964	853,438	Building of high-speed trains
New Tokyo International Airport Corporation	July 1966	244,991	Building, management of Narita Airport
Honshū-Shikoku Bridge Authority	July 1970	467,119	Building, management of toll roads and railroads linking Honshū and Shikoku
Japan Sewage Works Agency	November 1972	1,760,526	Building, rebuilding, designing of sewer facilities
The Japan Regional Development Corporation[b]	August 1974	1,760,526	Underground "New Town" building, development of industrial parks, mining areas

Source: Compiled from the Internet homepages of the corporations listed.

a. Scale is taken from corporations' financial plans for 2000.

b. Merged entity: date is for original establishment, not merger.

Table 3-7. *Gross Fixed Capital Formation as Share of GDP*
Percent

Country	1975	1997
Japan	5.29	5.73
United States	2.12	1.88
United Kingdom	4.75	1.40
Germany	3.87	2.00
France	3.71	2.83

Source: Compiled from *OECD National Accounts.*

which was much larger than the 1.88 percent of GDP in the United States and the 2 percent of GDP in Germany.

Table 3-8 shows that most of the general government gross fixed capital outlays went to local governments. In 1997, the combination of the Japanese government's final consumption expenditure and gross fixed capital formation as a percentage of GDP was the smallest of the top five developed nations. Among the five nations, this indication of the size of the Japanese government as the smallest, in conjunction with a fixed capital structure that is the largest, highlights the importance of its public works.

The Decay of the Construction State

Certainly public works spending to construct and maintain infrastructure was necessary during Japan's modernization and industrialization process, and marginal productivity was high for projects such as the Tōmei and Meishin Highways, which were built during the high-growth period. Expenditure on roads was important because it ensured the continuous flow of goods necessary for high growth and advanced regional industrialization. It also supported employment in weakened provinces abandoned by the industrialization and modernization process. These measures showcased politicians such as Kei Hara and Kakuei Tanaka as capable and dynamic leaders who embodied widespread democracy and Japanese modernization.

The completion of the construction state and the resulting equalization of employment levels between cities and villages stabilized society despite the rapid and robust growth of the high-growth period. In 1955, Soviet-type socialism was still a possibility. Therefore, policies had been chosen to achieve political stability through high growth, and as the economy expanded the resulting benefits were distributed somewhat evenly with the

Table 3-8. *Fixed Capital Formation Allocation,*
Central and Local Governments, 1997
Percent of GDP

Allocation	Japan	United States	United Kingdom	Germany	France
Final government consumption	9.74	15.21	20.94	19.41	19.33
Central government	2.28	5.74	13.40	2.17	9.89
Local government	7.35	9.47	7.38	9.66	5.46
Transfer[a]	7.66	3.67	8.32	4.33	1.58
Gross fixed capital formation	5.73	1.88	1.40	2.00	2.83
Central government	0.91	0.22	0.57	0.28	0.51
Local governments	4.76	1.66	0.83	1.68	1.96
Total	15.47	17.09	22.34	21.41	22.16

Source: Compiled from *OECD National Accounts.*
a. From the central government to other government departments.

aim of creating affluent and conservative local constituencies. Clearly, this political stability was made possible by the deliberate actions of the conservative alliance in 1955, which created the Liberal Democratic Party.

Past success, however, is the main reason for present failure. The structure of the construction state, which was built up over a long period of time, eventually disintegrated and became a hindrance not only to politics but also to economics. As illustrated in table 3-9, the productivity of public works has greatly declined in the last twenty years and is very close to zero, while the public works share of GDP for the provinces continues to increase. Even the provinces and farm villages that originally benefited from these funds are affected by the decrease in productivity because they must now pay a portion of the public works expenditure themselves. As a breeding ground for vested interests, the construction state system has

Table 3-9. *Marginal Productivity of Social Overhead Capital*

Period	Coefficient	Period	Coefficient
1955–59	0.247	1975–79	0.094
1960–64	0.322	1980–84	0.072
1965–69	0.361	1985–89	0.062
1970–74	0.180	1990–93	0.059

Source: Naoyuki Yoshino and Takanobu Nakajima, eds., *Kōkyōtōshi no Kēizaikōka* (Tokyo: Nihon Hyōronsha, 1999), p. 26.

merit only for construction companies and politicians who want to maintain the system for political reasons.

However, the time of *zoku* politicians[13] conducting Japan's politics should be over. This is why the Koizumi government is emphasizing the road budget, special funds, and public road works as important targets of structural reform. This creative destruction is necessary in order to move beyond Japanese modernization and build a twenty-first century system.

13. *Zoku* literally means tribe. *Zoku* politicians are those who are deeply involved in vested interests in specific sectors, such as roads and medical care.

4 From Structural Reform to Institutional Reform

In the 130 years after the Meiji Restoration, Japan had successfully completed the modernization and industrialization of its economy and society, creating a political and administrative system with a public construction state at its core. In a previous book, I analyzed the system of capitalism in Japan and described it as a mixed economy "beyond capitalism"; this system could also be called "Japanese capitalism."[1]

Global capitalism has now begun a transformation toward a postmodern system. Although it is unclear what the result of this transformation will be, what is apparent is that as global capitalism transforms itself, Japanese capitalism must adapt to this new environment. The desirability, or rather necessity, of this adaptation is currently being debated in terms of the need for structural reform. What this structural reform will entail should be clearly defined

1. Eisuke Sakakibara, *Beyond Capitalism: The Japanese Model of Market Economics* (Lanham, Md.: University Press of America, Economic Strategy Institute, 1993), chap. 2, pp. 4–11, and chapter 4, pp. 67–124.

to illustrate which elements of the system should be changed and which should be retained.

Structure of Japanese Capitalism

In general, the word *structure* refers to social and cultural relationships and institutions that do not change with time or place. Alternatively, it can refer to systemic characteristics affected only by geographic location or weather. While structuralists like Levi-Strauss thought the former definition correct, historians like Fernand Braudel believed the latter—structure refers to that which is affected by factors that change only very slowly:

> The second key, which is more useful, is the word "structure." Whether for good or bad, it controls the issue of long-term continuation. Observers of social realism understand structure as a fixed relationship between social reality and the masses that is organized and closely tied together. To us historians, structure is something that is brought together and combined in a precise way, but more than that, it refers to a reality that continues for a very long time without fading. Some structures have long lives and become permanent characteristics for countless generations. In other words, some structures stop the tide of history, agitate it, and then control it. Others disintegrate much faster. However, all structures are obstacles at the same time they are supports. Structures as obstacles should be thought of as a limit that humans and their experiences cannot overcome. Think of how difficult it is to break the framework of physics, certain biological realities, limits of productivity, or any type of psychological barrier. Emotional frameworks are also prisons that are maintained long term. The most approachable is the example of physical limitation. Over centuries, people have been preoccupied with nature, food distribution, animal husbandry, farming, and the balance that is gradually created among these. If one tries to rethink everything, it all becomes uncertain and it becomes difficult to extricate oneself. Think of the impressively constant migration to the cities, the constancy of roads and delivery, and the geographic framework of civilizations.[2]

2. Kōji Inoue, *Ferunan Burodel* (Tokyo: Shinhyōron, 1989), p. 26 (my translation).

However, the definition of structure in the context of structural reform is quite different from Braudel's conceptualization of structures that emerge slowly and disintegrate equally slowly. In this book, structures refer to political, economic and social systems or procedures that can be reformed through various policies in the medium term. In the context of the global transformation toward a postmodern economic system, there exist numerous archaic and malfunctioning institutions and procedures that have not adjusted to the changes in this environment. These institutions and procedures can, and should, be reformed by policies in the short to medium term.

Although structural reform can be affected by or achieved through the efforts of individuals and corporations, for the sake of clarity the discussion here will be limited to public policy. The government's policy instruments for implementing structural reform include the modification of laws and regulations (including those of the Constitution) in areas such as the tax code; the composition of central and local government budgets; and the application of administrative and political procedures within the government and the Diet. Four types of structural reforms need to be carried out through these policy instruments.

The first type should be economic reform, in the form of either deregulation or re-regulation. The dual structure of the economy must be dissolved to increase productivity. This can be accomplished through changes in laws, regulations, and "administrative guidance" (see note 12, below), as well as through modifications of the budget, such as the reduction of subsidies and changes in tax policy.

The second type should be political and administrative reform such that the political dual structure, which is closely tied to the economic dual structure, dissolves. Indeed, the main purpose of this chapter is to show the deep connection between these two dual structures and in so doing, demonstrate the significance of increasing economic productivity through the structural reform of both. Political and administrative reform can be carried out through modifications of laws and regulations, including constitutional, civil, criminal, administrative, and parliamentary law reform, as well as reform of related regulations and changes to political and administrative processes.

The third and fourth types of structural reform should be social reforms achieved through legal and administrative changes in education and immigration, respectively. Japan must urgently reform its education policy. The Ministry of Education and Science's systematic implementation of poor education policy reforms has resulted in declining scholastic achievement, even at the university level; Japanese education is now in an appalling state. Policy reforms can be rapidly implemented through fundamental changes in the School Education Law, as well as related laws and regulations. (Education policy is discussed further in chapter 8.)

In terms of immigration, reforms should reverse Japan's isolationist tendencies, as reflected in laws such as the Nationality Act and Immigration Act, and make the country more open. This would be the third "opening of the nation," the objective of which is to prepare Japan for globalization. With the opening of the nation, there must also be reform in the conduct of foreign policy. (These issues are discussed in chapter 7.)

Of course, as noted in Braudel's discussion of slowly changing structures, deeply rooted elements of history and culture cannot be changed through policy instruments, either in the short or medium term. Attempts to modify such unchangeable elements would result in confusion and systemic destruction. Structural reform does not imply changes in traditional Japanese culture or customs, nor does it herald the wholesale adoption of U.S. standards. Rather, it is an attempt to adapt Japanese capitalism to a new environment. The unchangeable parts of the system would continue to exist, but other institutions and procedures would change over time, either purposefully through policy efforts or through pressure from the worldwide evolution to a postmodern economy. Any system that emerged from structural reform would adapt to a globalized world while remaining distinctly Japanese.

Dissolution of the Old Dual Economic Structure

Historically, the dual structure of the Japanese economy referred to the wage and income disparity between modern and pre-modern industries. Yonosuke Gotō of the Economic Planning Agency proposed this concept during a 1957 debate about high-growth policy with Osamu Shimomura, a trusted adviser to former Prime Minister Hayato Ikeda and well-known advocate of high-growth policy.[3] Gotō, as well as others, noted that the dual structure of the economy was one of the adverse results of the high-growth policy.

Marxist Kazuji Nagasu argued that since the Meiji era, the dual structure of modern and pre-modern industries had been a fundamental characteristic of the Japanese economy, and within this dual structure lay the extreme

3. Osamu Shimomura, *Kēzaisēchō Jitsugen no Tameni* (Tokyo: Kōchikai, 1958), pp. 227–312.

stratification of the industrial structure, which was dominated by monopolistic enterprises and supported by pre-modern subsidiaries. According to
Nagasu, the economy had been characterized by wage and productivity differentials, as well as disparity in capital intensity.[4] High growth through capital accumulation only led to a widening of these disparities. This exacer-
bated the gap in the dual structure and in the capitalist system generally,
making the dissolution of the dual structure impossible.

Non-Marxists like Miyohei Shinohara agreed with Nagasu on the actual
existence of the dual structure, but argued that its dissolution, while complicated, was possible through industrial and agricultural revolution. Shinohara noted that the "sustainability of [Japan's] high growth rate depends
upon whether the structural transition associated with reaching the stage of
a developed economy will proceed smoothly."[5]

Fortunately, the structural transition was achieved relatively smoothly
between 1955 and the mid-1970s via the industrial and agricultural revolution Shinohara described. Due to the dramatic decline in the percentage
of the labor force engaged in agriculture and the rapid development of
export-oriented manufacturing, agricultural and manufacturing labor productivity increased between threefold and fourfold from 1960 to 1980, as
illustrated in table 4-1. Over time, the disparities in wages and income
gradually shrank, despite Marxist (and other) predictions of catastrophe.

The employment displacement caused by the agricultural revolution has
been eased through both the implementation of policies developed specifically for the agriculture industry and increased investment in the provinces
under the auspices of the public construction state. The agriculture industry in particular has been heavily subsidized by the government, as have
rural areas generally: the Japanese government has used income policies,
such as the rice subsidy, as an income transfer mechanism from the urban
manufacturing wage earner to the rural farmer. The government has also
supported rural areas through intensive public investment to ensure employment security.

Primarily because of these government policies, the lower income level
of agricultural households and the higher income level of nonagricultural
households switched positions in 1972; the income of the former now
exceeds that of the latter by a substantial margin. The average annual

4. Kazuji Nagasu, *Nihon Kēzai Nyūmon* (Tokyo: Kōbunsha, 1960), pp. 182–86.
5. Miyohei Shinohara, *Kōdo Seichō no Himitsu* (Tokyo: Nihon Kēzai Shinbunsha, 1961), p. 93
(my translation).

Table 4-1. *Relative Labor Productivity in the Japanese Economy*
Index, 1980 = 100

	Productivity		Employment		Labor productivity	
Year	Agri-culture	Manu-facturing	Agri-culture	Manu-facturing	Agri-culture	Manu-facturing
1960	76.3	19.2	239.3	69.2	31.9	27.7
1965	85.4	32.5	196.6	84.1	43.4	38.6
1980	100.0	100.0	100.0	100.0	100.0	100.0
1985	110.3	118.6	87.2	106.3	126.5	111.6
1990	105.9	147.9	77.3	110.1	137.0	134.4
1995	101.0	141.8	63.9	106.5	158.1	133.2
2000	94.9	140.9	55.8	96.6	170.1	145.8

Source: Compiled by author using data from the websites of the Ministry of Agriculture, Forestry, and Fisheries; Ministry of Economy, Trade, and Industry; and Ministry of Public Management, Home Affairs, Posts and Telecommunications.

income of an agricultural household in 1998 was ¥8.68 million, with income strictly from agriculture accounting for 15 percent of that amount.[6] This is in comparison to the ¥7.07 million of a nonagricultural wage earner's household. The situation is similar with regard to accumulated wealth. Gross savings of an average agricultural household is ¥29.8 million, which is 2.4 times greater than that of a nonagricultural wage earner's household, while average debt of the former is ¥3.27 million, which is 65 percent of that of a wage earner's household.

The establishment of the public construction state during the high-growth period enabled the government to succeed in cushioning the blow to the agricultural sector and to rural areas, which allowed the dissolution of the old dual structure while simultaneously modernizing and industrializing the economy.

New Dual Structure of Japanese Economics

As wage and income disparity among industries and corporations of varying size disappeared along with the old dual structure, a new duality among industries emerged. While the old dual structure was characterized by

---

6. Most agricultural households in Japan are now part time; that is, they have at least one household member employed outside the farm. This issue is discussed further in chapter 10.

income and wage differentials, the new dual structure is based on differences in productivity.

The Japanese economy can currently be divided into two sectors: the export-oriented manufacturing sector, which has a high level of productivity and is globally competitive, and the domestic manufacturing and service sectors, which have a low level of productivity and are protected by regulations and subsidies.[7] The former, represented by firms such as Sony and Toyota, are engaged in the export of products manufactured in the automotive, electronics, machine tool, and steel industries. The latter are engaged in the domestic manufacturing of foodstuffs, textiles, and furniture and in providing domestic retail, construction, and medical services, respectively.[8]

According to a recent McKinsey report, the share of employment in export-oriented manufacturing is approximately 10 percent, and its average productivity is estimated to be 120 percent of that of the United States.[9] In contrast, the domestic service sector accounts for approximately 75 percent of employment, while its productivity is estimated to be only 63 percent of that of the United States.[10] Domestic manufacturing accounts for approximately 15 percent of employment, and its productivity is also estimated to be 63 percent of that of the United States.[11] The average productivity of the domestic service and manufacturing sectors is less than two-thirds of that of these sectors in the United States.

The question that arises from these data is why the domestic manufacturing and service sectors perform so poorly despite a substantial infusion of public money. Chapter 6 provides a detailed discussion of the problems associated with balance sheet and nonperforming asset problems; for the purpose of this discussion it is sufficient to note that the poor performance of the domestic manufacturing and service sectors is endemic to those sectors' stagnation, not because of problems in the financial institutions from which they borrow. Japan must, therefore, implement structural reform in these stagnant sectors if it is to overcome long-term recession. As discussed

---

7. Although domestic manufacturing and services are two separate sectors, they are grouped as one at times for the purpose of this discussion.

8. Although not usually included, agriculture and construction are added in the service sector here.

9. McKinsey Global Institute, *Why the Japanese Economy Is Not Growing: Micro Barriers to Productivity Growth* (Washington: McKinsey Global Institute, 2000), Executive Summary, Exhibit 3, p. 8.

10. Ibid.

11. Ibid.

earlier, the policy instruments available for carrying out such reform are implementation of new legislation, revision of laws and regulations related to these sectors, reallocation of parts of the budget, and changes to related practices, such as "administrative guidance."[12]

What particular laws or budget allocations are necessary for such reform? Due to the sector-specific nature of this structural reform, specific measures differ from industry to industry. The following analysis of the retail industry, based on the McKinsey study, illustrates the problems and possible solutions.[13]

In the retail industry, which accounts for 12 percent of employment and 5 percent of GDP, labor productivity is calculated to be 50 percent of that in the United States. Japan has a high percentage of traditional small businesses, which account for 55 percent of total labor hours, as compared to 19 percent of the U.S. total and 26 percent of France's.[14] By contrast, the share of labor hours for large-scale stores, such as discounters, general merchandise stores and supermarkets, is 12 percent as compared with 35 percent in the United States. The labor productivity index of the traditional retail sector in Japan is 19 compared with 57 in the United States. The labor productivity of Japanese supermarkets is also significantly lower (only 73 versus 122 for U.S. supermarkets). Market penetration by foreign firms is generally negligible in the retail sector and in some subsectors is less than 1 percent.

The causes of stagnant labor productivity are a lack of transparency and information about price and quality, as well as a lack of competition due to various entry and exit barriers.[15] These barriers to entry and exit are created and maintained through regulation, favorable tax treatment, and subsidies. For example, entry restrictions are stipulated in the Large-Scale Retail Location Law, which states that the construction of stores over 1,000 square meters can be approved only after taking into consideration environmental protection and city planning concerns. Local committees, including

12. "Administrative guidance" (*gyosei shidou*) is a suggestion or recommendation by an administrative agency advising an individual or a business to carry out or not carry out a certain action. Although not legally binding, it is sometimes related to the interpretation of a law or laws. It is often issued verbally but must be put into writing if requested by the person(s) receiving the guidance.

13. McKinsey, *Why the Japanese Economy Is Not Growing*, chap. 4, "Sector Case Studies: Retailing," pp. 1–41. Statistics are from Exhibit 1, p. 26, and Exhibits 3 and 4, p. 27.

14. In the McKinsey study these are described as "non-chained small stores often managed by a family" (ibid., Exhibit 2, p. 26).

15 Ibid., Executive Summary, pp. 3–4.

local small business owners, deliberate over the request, and then the prefecture and local governments make their final decision based on the deliberations. The revision of the law in 2000 localized the decisionmaking mechanism and eliminated the role of the central government, which has resulted in a de facto strengthening of the entry barrier.[16] The Urban Redevelopment Law is another barrier to entry. The law cedes authority to local governments to approve large-scale development in urban areas as long as two-thirds of the residents are in agreement, and the local governments ordinarily do not give approval unless consensus is reached in the community.[17] Meanwhile, low property taxes exert little pressure on traditional stores to exit the market, a high capital gains tax acts as a deterrent to the sale of land, and the inheritance tax deduction encourages the holding of land. For example, the Inheritance Tax Law has a special provision that allows small-scale shopkeepers to deduct 80 percent of the inheritance value from the taxable amount for land only. Since most small businesses qualify for this special provision, families tend to hold on to their land and their stores, even if they expect to derive no profit from the business.[18]

The government has also made certain budget allocations that are favorable to, and create significant exit barriers for, retail shops. In 1998, the government began to provide what would eventually amount to ¥30 trillion in loan guarantees to small businesses with almost no credit evaluation. Small retailers account for 13 percent, or ¥4 trillion, of this amount. The Town Center Revitalization Law enacted in 1998 has a budget of ¥1 trillion annually to be used to reinvigorate town centers.[19] As a result, many shopping arcades have been built with free parking areas using this budget. These measures have been enacted in the name of assisting small- and medium-sized businesses, but in fact they have resulted in creating exit barriers to small, inefficient retail stores.

These tax and budget measures, which are taken to protect the weak, are intended to preserve stability rather than promote efficiency. Safety nets are necessary even in market economies and some social democratic measures can be justified on these grounds. However, the problem in Japan is that these measures are not the exception but the rule in most of the domestic manufacturing and service industries, which together account for 90 percent of employment in Japan.

16, Ibid., chap. 4, "Sector Case Studies: Retailing," pp. 9–10.

17. Ibid., chap. 4, "Sector Case Studies: Retailing," p. 11.

18. Ibid., chap. 4, "Sector Case Studies: Retailing," pp. 12–13.

19. Ibid., chap. 4, "Sector Case Studies: Retailing," p. 13.

Thus market principles apply mainly to export-oriented industries, which account for only 10 percent of employment, while more socialist principles apply to the industries that account for 90 percent of employment. While similar socialist policies were prevalent in Western Europe through the 1970s, the Thatcher Revolution and European integration have effectively abolished many of the old industrial subsidies and protections. Even the more social democratic governments in Europe that have advocated a "third path" are not promoting the reintroduction of industrial protection; rather, they seek to make market principles compatible with a social welfare system. Japan is the only Group of Seven country that retains a system characterized more by socialist than market principles. Ironically, it is Japan's "conservative" LDP that has nurtured the political and administrative institutions that facilitate this socialist economy. The dual political structure and its relationship to the dual economic structure provide an explanation for this.

Dual Structure of Japanese Politics

The fact that one part of the Japanese dual economic system adheres to socialist principles supported by political and administrative institutions, as well as by the policymaking process, implies that its dissolution is not possible without fundamental changes in political and administrative structures. Parallel to the economic system in Japan is the political system, which has also developed a dual structure over many years. Just as the economic dual structure is characterized by the coexistence of market mechanisms and socialist policies, the political dual structure has its counterparts in the parliamentary government and socialist party systems.

Japan is the only country among developed democracies where the party plays such a disproportionately significant role in policymaking. Party policymaking organs, such as the Council for Policy Coordination, the General Council, and the various committees and research groups of the LDP, do not exist in the United States or in Western Europe. Party organizations in those countries primarily engage in elections, and ministers, secretaries, or political appointees formulate policy.

The United Kingdom provides a relevant illustration of the differences between Japan and other developed democracies. In enacting government legislation, the cabinet and ministers first conceive a legislative idea, which bureaucrats turn into a concrete legislative program. Parliamentary draftsmen then write the legislation in consultation with departmental lawyers, and the result is submitted to the government. Approximately 70 to 80 percent of annual legislation is made up of such bills. Only party members with government portfolios are involved in the process, as other party members' participation is thought to be against the rules of democratic procedure.

The government is a strong force in the parliament and continues to lead even after the submission of the government's bill or budget. In some cases, only the prime minister and a few relevant people know the details of the budget or legislation until it is submitted. In the Treasury, it is not only the chancellor of the exchequer but also several junior ministers who play a central role in compiling the budget. However, it is not until the chancellor delivers the budget speech that all of the details of the government's budget become public. Party politicians who are not in the government have no involvement, particularly in the case of the budget. The process is intended to eliminate any inappropriate influence by politicians while the government is drafting the budget. Politicians without government portfolios do participate in parliamentary discussions as backbenchers but they do not, or more accurately cannot, involve themselves in the decisionmaking process of the government budget.

This separation between the government and other members of parliament can be seen in how the United Kingdom traditionally regards government ministers and officials as "His or Her Majesty's servants," while other parliamentary representatives are regarded as "private members of Parliament." The two groups, the government and the party politicians, are not supposed to work side-by-side on policymaking. Ministers are expected to carry out explanation and consultation with private members. This traditional rule is based on the premise that the government is run by the ministers, the numbers of which exceed 100. In countries like Germany, France, and the United States, the party politicians do not play a central role in drafting the government's budget or bills.

In Japan, neither the secretary general of the party, the chairman of the Policy Coordinating Council, nor the chairmen of the various committees and research groups have any legal authority to draft government legislation. Neither do these individuals or entities have any legal requirements for disclosure of any internal election process. Since these entities and individuals do not have any legal authority to draft government plans, they cannot be prosecuted for illegal activities such as bribery even if they receive contributions from vested interests. Indeed, there are some countries where the party wields very strong leverage in policymaking; however, these are communist countries, such as China and Vietnam.

When a Japanese ministry prepares the draft of a bill, it consults with or receives instruction from the corresponding party committee or research group from an early stage. When the details of the draft are agreed upon between the committee or the research group and the ministry, the bill is then submitted to the Council for Policy Coordination. After the approval by the council, the General Council gives the final approval. In the current coalition government, coordination among the secretaries-general and the chairmen of the various policy councils proceeds simultaneously and in parallel with the above-mentioned process in the LDP.

The party plays a similar role in drafting the government budget, but with one difference. Under Prime Minister Koizumi's government, the Council for Fiscal and Economic Affairs has been created to facilitate the formulation of the general framework for the budget, which is the only change from the past. This was an attempt to increase the power of the prime minister and his office in the budget process, which is an important part of structural reform. When the normal session of the Diet adjourns in late June or early July, each ministry engages in an annual reshuffling of personnel. The budget process begins in the various ministries on the night after the reshuffling and requests are subsequently submitted to the Ministry of Finance. Between September and the end of December, details of the requests are decided upon after complex negotiations between the requesting ministry, the Ministry of Finance, and the corresponding party committee or research group. The Council for Policy Coordination and the General Council play significant roles in the drafting of budget legislation. For example, the chairman of the Council for Policy Coordination participates in the final negotiation of details between the two ministers involved. With regard to coalition parties, the secretaries-general and the chairmen of policy coordinating councils play similar roles, as in the case of other legislation.

This active involvement of party members without government portfolios in the details of budget drafting is unique to Japan, and it is a procedure that was established in the late 1960s and early 1970s during the latter phase of the high economic growth period. There are several reasons for the development of this unique process. One is single party dominance. The second is the strength of the Diet relative to the government, which allows the Diet to involve itself in the process without waiting for the government,

Norihiko Narita argues.[20] This is in contrast with the United Kingdom, where the government does not have to coordinate with the parliament before submission of the budget or other legislation. Then, after its submission, the government ministers take strong leadership roles in the parliamentary discussion.

Among most developed democracies where the rule of law prevails, politicians without legal authority cannot, under normal circumstances, directly involve themselves in the government's decisionmaking with regard to the drafting of legislation or the budget. Japan is the only exception. In this sense, there is something missing in Japan's democracy. It is the lack of pervasiveness of the rule of law, or the lack of codification of the roles of various groups, as manifested in the lack of accountability in Japan's policymaking process. This lack of accountability is a symptom of Japan's political dual structure, which coexists with the economic dual structure.

Interaction between the Two Dual Structures

The two dual structures of the political and economic systems interact with each other in the policymaking process through representatives of vested interests and politicians of various party committees and research groups. These politicians have often been called *zoku,* or "tribe parliamentarians." Within the confines of the Political Contribution Act, as long as politicians do not occupy government positions by becoming ministers or state secretaries and as long as they do not use their legal right to question the legislation in the Diet, they are free to interact with vested interests. This also covers receiving financial contributions from vested interests. As mentioned previously, politicians cannot be prosecuted for bribery because they do not possess the legal authority to influence government. Government bureaucrats in charge of specific issues are also co-opted in this policymaking process to the extent that legal constraints allow.

The retail industry provides an illustrative case of the interaction of the dual political and economic structures. Loans with government guarantees of up to ¥30 trillion were expanded to small- and medium-sized enterprises in 1998. The key players in this expansion were the Ministry of

20. Norihiko Narita, "Gikai ni Okeru Kaiha to sono Yakuwari: Nihon to Shōgaikoku," *Reference* (August 1998), pp. 10–11, 22–23.

International Trade and Industry (MITI), which is the predecessor of the Ministry of Economy, Trade, and Industry (METI), the Commerce Committee of the LDP, and the various associations of small and medium enterprises. The ministerial division in charge of the issue was the Finance Division of the Medium to Small Enterprises Agency. The loan guarantees were administered through regional credit guarantee associations, which have chapters across the country.

The official reason for the institution of the measure was to avoid a credit crunch in the midst of a financial crisis. As a measure to circumvent a credit crunch, it was effective, requiring only a relatively small addition of capital to the guarantee associations. The sum was relatively small, assuming the loans did not become nonperforming assets. The measure also managed to keep inefficient retailers that otherwise would have exited the market in business. It is possible to argue that socialist measures are necessary to cushion the effects of a recession. However, the exit of inefficient enterprises from the market during economic downturns is an important mechanism of a functioning market economy.

In addition to expanding the loan guarantee limit in 1998, the government began allocating an annual budget of more than ¥1 trillion to local shopping communities to construct shopping arcades and other projects. Public financial institutions, such as the Japan Development Bank (the current Development Bank of Japan) and others, mobilized to ease the credit crunch, which led to an increase of their nonperforming assets. While the move to ease the credit crunch vis-à-vis investment in small- and medium-sized enterprises was politically clever, it was economically illogical. The potential public disapproval of a huge infusion of public money into the banking sector may have been offset by the benefits to small and medium enterprises, but the concept of financing the structural reform of banks while guaranteeing loans to inefficient businesses is logically inconsistent. This inconsistency is the result of the workings of the "iron triangle" of politicians, bureaucracy, and vested interests.

In addition to the loan guarantees, the influence of the iron triangle can be found in the agricultural land irrigation projects. The FY2000 budget for projects implemented by both the central and local governments was roughly ¥3 trillion, ¥1.1 trillion of which was for local government subsidies. The expenditure on agricultural and farm village infrastructure, which includes irrigation, is the largest item in the Ministry of Agriculture, Forestry, and Fisheries (MAFF) budget, accounting for roughly

Table 4-2. *Ministry of Agriculture, Forestry, and Fisheries (MAFF)*
Expenditures
Millions of yen, except as indicated

Type of expenditure	1960	1970	1980	1990	1999
Total general account (GA) budget	1,765,163	8,213,085	43,681,367	69,651,178	89,018,897
MAFF budget	138,641	885,059	3,108,025	2,518,812	2,939,080
Percentage of GA budget	7.85	10.78	7.12	3.62	3.30
Agricultural and farm village infra-structure	38,772	181,291	862,059	993,356	1,378,860
Percentage of MAFF budget	27.97	20.48	27.74	39.44	46.91
Price stabilization of agricultural products	31,200	393,292	773,202	311,455	366,856
Percentage of MAFF budget	22.50	44.44	24.88	12.37	12.48
Other	68,669	310,476	1,472,764	1,214,001	1,193,364
Percentage of MAFF budget	49.53	35.08	47.39	48.20	40.60

Source: Japan, Ministry of Agriculture, Forestry and Fisheries, *Shokyryō Nōgyō Nōson Hakusho Fuzoku Tōkeihyo* (Tokyo, 1999), pp. 176–77.

one half. The aggregate budget for the MAFF has been dwindling since 1980, due to a decline in expenditure for the stabilization of prices of agricultural products, yet infrastructure expenditures have been increasing, as illustrated in table 4-2. Part of the reason is that behind such annual budgets lie long-term irrigation plans, one of which has an expected expenditure of ¥41 trillion for the period 1993 to 2006. This mechanism of long-term projects supporting annual budgets is typical and can be found in other public investment areas such as roads and port construction.

Such an inefficient system is possible because of the way in which the iron triangle operates. Nationally, there are approximately 7,000 associations for agricultural land irrigation with a membership of approximately 4 million. Their counterparts are the Committee for Agriculture and Fisheries and the Research Group for Comprehensive Agricultural Policy of the LDP. In the bureaucracy, the Management Bureau (the former Structural Reform Bureau) of the MAFF is in charge of irrigation projects. The Bureau nominates a candidate from the LDP, usually an ex-bureaucrat, in every upper house election and gets him or her elected with the support of the agricultural land irrigation associations. After the ex-bureaucrat is elected, he serves as an adviser to the National Association for Agricultural Land Irrigation and as an executive director for the Political Association for Agricultural Land Irrigation. The local associations for agricultural land irrigation are quite influential in getting contracts awarded to their projects; as a result of this highly politicized process, the number of construction companies has increased and reached more than 610,000 in 2000 despite the decade-long recession. The number of people employed in the construction industry in the same year was 6.53 million; clearly many of these companies are only employing a few people.

Furthermore, the construction period of these projects typically spans more than twenty years. A local area's employment level and economic well-being depends upon these projects, yet they are often rendered obsolete before they are finished. Indeed, many projects survive with some moderate changes even after it is realized they no longer serve any purpose because there are no clear-cut rules for the suspension or scaling down of projects, such as reallocating costs between central and local governments.

The recently revealed modifications to, and final suspension of, the Nakaumi Reclamation and Desalination Project constitute one example. As illustrated in table 4-3, this project was launched in the Honjō district in 1963 with the objective of reclaiming land for rice production. The original justification for the project disappeared as early as 1970, when the Ministry of Agriculture shifted from a policy of increasing to reducing rice production and restraining new investment in agricultural land. However, the project survived by revising its objective to that of reclaiming land for other crops, despite farmers' protests. Between 1989 and 1992, construction in four districts, including Yumihama and Hikona, was completed. The local governments of the Honjō district explicitly opposed the continuation of the project in 1996, but the project was suspended only after four more years of negotiation between the central and local governments, a full thirty-seven years after it was launched.

The Nakaumi Project is not atypical—the revision and prolongation of projects is quite common. Although such projects contribute to employment in rural areas, pursuing extensive irrigation projects in the face of a reduction in rice production and a liberalization policy is illogical. Rather than revitalizing rural areas, the continuation of unnecessary projects

Table 4-3. *Historical Evolution of the Nakaumi Reclamation and Desalination Project*

Year	Event
1963	Launch of Nakaumi Project amid calls for increased production of foodstuffs
1968	Construction begins to accelerate
1969	Shift in agricultural policy from increased to decreased production; original objective lost
1974	Completion of Nakaumi Floodgate
1981	Completion of Moriyama Dike; Honjo District now surrounded by dikes
1982	Association of Local Residents to Protect Environment formed (changed to Association of Local Residents to Protect Beautiful Nakaumi in 1995)
1984	Plan for reclaimed land changed from rice production to other crops
1987	Ministry of Agriculture, Forestry, and Fisheries request Shimane and Tottori prefectures to experiment with limited desalination
1988	Governors of Shimane and Tottori prefectures request postponement of desalination
1989	Construction completed in three districts, including Yumihama (Tottori) and Aki (Shimane)
1992	Construction in Hikone District completed
1995	Governor of Shimane announces that reclamation will move forward
1996	City assemblies of Sakaiminato and Yonago and mayor of Yonago request suspension from Shimane governor; after Shimane governor requests the ministry to resume construction, the coalition, Socialist and Liberal Democratic parties, and Sakigake conduct research to decide whether to postpone the decision for two years
1999	Committee of the Consultative Council for the Ministry of Agriculture, Forestry, and Fisheries is formed to study the Honjo District Project
2000	Final suspension of construction in Honjo District

Source: Compiled by author from various sources, including newspapers and journals.

favoring specific politically active construction companies will, in the long run, lead to a faster decline in Japanese agriculture.

Party-Bureaucracy Complex and Consequences for Reform

As can be seen in the examples of agricultural land irrigation projects, the party (the "tribe parliamentarians") and the bureaucracy have an overly close alliance. This party-bureaucracy complex is possible because of the dual nature of the political structure. Bureaucrats in each ministry develop long-lasting, close relationships with the tribe parliamentarians, ties that are usually much stronger than the bureaucrats' ties to their own ministers. Thus ministers, whose average tenure has been less than a year during the past few decades, have much less leverage over the bureaucracy than the party's tribe parliamentarians.

In contrast to the close relationship between the party and the bureaucracy, long-standing mistrust characterizes the relationship between the party and the government. This antagonism is largely historical. During the late nineteenth century, the roots of the modern Japanese political system were established when the government was formed by the victors of the Meiji Restoration, who were former samurai from Satsuma and Choshu, and the opposition party was formed by the losers, who were samurai from Tosa, Saga, and other feudal domains. The antagonism between the two groups has turned into a long-term power struggle between the government and the party.

Under the democratic system, the legislature, administration, and judiciary are the three key public entities. Elected officials run the legislature, while the prime minister, ministers, junior ministers, political appointees, and career bureaucrats run the administration, or government. The government formulates policies, which the legislature considers for enactment along with those proposed by the representatives themselves. There is no official role for the party in the policymaking process before the legislation goes to the parliament. The major function of the party is to win elections and make its candidate prime minister. (However, once the prime minister is elected as the head of government, policymaking should be 100 percent the prime minister's domain.) Parties still play an important role in the legislature: they deliberate and decide on legislation and the budget. However, they do so only as members of the public institution of the legislature.

Some may argue that it is only natural for bureaucrats to develop relationships with politicians in view of the bureaucrats' desire for favorable legislation. However, in countries such as the United Kingdom, an intimate association is effectively barred from the policy process because allowing consultation between politicians without government portfolios and bureaucrats would taint the integrity of the policy process. In a parliamentary democracy, elected politicians in the government should lead policymaking; politicians who want to be involved in the drafting of the budget or other legislation should either propose legislation or become prime ministers, ministers, junior ministers or political appointees. Those who do not should debate and vote on what the government has already submitted to the Diet.

In Japan, the decisionmaking mechanism tends to lack transparency and is thus not firmly rooted in the rule of law. A system firmly based on the rule of law should have the roles of the party, government, and bureaucracy codified in law. The party in Japan is essentially a private entity that has created a large, opaque, and quasi-official policy process in association with the bureaucracy, despite the fact that it has no legal authority to do so. This is not an appropriate mechanism for democratic leadership. Moreover, genuine leadership by elected officials, which should be the case in a parliamentary democracy, has become difficult under the current system because policymaking by the Cabinet and the prime minister can be, and often has been, blocked by the alliance of the party and the bureaucracy. Under such a system, it is difficult for the prime minister or the cabinet to take the lead in policymaking.

Dissolving the Dual Structure

Japan needs to immediately address structural reform vis-à-vis the dismantling of the two dual structures. The Japanese economic and political systems are very similar to those of socialist countries. Socialist elements in the economy have been maintained through regulation, budget, and tax measures, while similar elements in the political system have been brought about through the intimate alliance between the dominant party and the bureaucracy. There needs to be a clearer and more effective effort to "marketize" the economic system and to democratize the political system. The issues that must be tackled are both institutional and sector specific in nature. Therefore, a case-by-case approach needs to be adopted. In each sector of the economy, there should be deregulation, a change in the allocation of the budget, a change in the tax code, and specific efforts to break down the party-bureaucracy complex.

An important factor in implementing these reforms is establishing unambiguous, strong leadership by the prime minister and cabinet ministers over the party and the bureaucracy. The average tenure of the prime minister and other ministers, which has been a year or less during the past decade, should be lengthened to at least four years. With tenure of only one to two years, ministers cannot effectively confront the iron triangle of the party, bureaucracy, and vested interests. With longer tenure, it would also be easier for the prime minister to have many more competent political appointees on his staff than in the past. The direct election of the prime minister might also be an effective way to strengthen the authority of the office and lengthen the tenure.

Strengthening the function and power of the prime minister's office to the level of that of the president of the United States or Korea has begun under Prime Minister Koizumi, and this must continue. Although there are differences between presidential and parliamentary systems, the strength of the executive in the presidential system should be incorporated into the Japanese political structure. It is also important to increase the number of staff directly appointed by the prime minister to strengthen his leadership. Having cabinet-level staff in the prime minister's office is essential. In addition, because of the dramatic increase in the number of complex issues that must be faced, it has become extremely important to have horizontal coordination among ministries, which span many jurisdictions. Making such changes is essential in order to break the party-bureaucracy complex. Only when the prime minister's staff of political appointees begins to show strong leadership can the stage be set for large-scale structural reform.

5 Development of Global Corporations

As mentioned before, Japan's era of modernization and industrialization can be divided into two stages: from the Meiji to the beginning of the Taisho period, when the classical capitalist system was formed during the shift in focus from Asia to Europe; and from the end of the Taisho period through the Showa period, when the new Japanese capitalist system gradually came into being. Similar to what occurred in much of the West, Japan's experience with the Great Depression and World War II led to a global shift from classical capitalism to a mixed economy. Yet within this broader trend, Japan's postwar process was unusual because there was complete corporate reform through disinvestments during the war and occupation. In addition, strong political and administrative support for regionalism, agriculturalism, and subsidies, as well as the establishment of unique regional communities and support for small- and medium-sized businesses, made Japan's process distinct.

The *Zaibatsu* and the Japanese Corporate System

Historically, the *zaibatsu*, which controlled Japanese industry during the Meiji and Taisho periods, began either as mining companies or as politically connected businesses in industries such as merchandising, financial services, and shipping. Sumitomo and Furukawa are examples of the former, while Mitsui, Mitsubishi, Yasuda, Okura, and Fujita are examples of the latter. The latter group of *zaibatsu* companies eventually expanded by investing assets from their political businesses in mines through offshoot companies such as Mitsui-Miike, Mitsubishi-Takashima, and Fujita-Kosaka. These *zaibatsu* solidified their foundations by the end of the Meiji period and continued to grow after World War I.

According to Hidemasa Morikawa, Japan's *zaibatsu* contained some distinctive characteristics compared with similar entities in other countries.[1] First, the affiliated *zaibatsu* families had little independence, and members were completely controlled by the combined family unit. Various branch families were not permitted to control their assets independent of the family council. (The family councils of the eleven Mitsui and thirteen Yasuda family branches were typical examples.) Second, the businesses were centered in modern industries and were diversified, in contrast with conglomerates around the world that were more interested in protecting existing assets. Third, management was given extensive authority. *Zaibatsu* founded earlier during the Meiji period, such as Sumitomo and Mitsui, had already given managerial authority to their chief executive officers (CEOs). Yet even in the new *zaibatsu*, when the founders retired, power shifted to professional CEOs. Hikojirō Nakamigawa, the nephew of Yukichi Fukuzawa and an alumnus of Keio University, created a group of Keio graduates who were Mitsui *zaibatsu* executives. Although the professional CEOs came from various backgrounds, they all went through institutions of higher education created since the Meiji period.

The educational meritocracy system, which had continued since the Meiji period, was one of the characteristics of modern Japan. In a sense, the predecessors to the postwar salaried executives were the prewar professional CEOs. During the Showa period, the professional executives gradually gained power and eventually took over from the founding industrialists. According to Yoshimatsu Aonuma, 50 percent of CEOs were owners in

1. Hidemasa Morikawa, *Nihon Zaibatsu Shi* (Tokyo: Kyōikusha, 1978) and *Nihon Kēē Shi* (Tokyo: Nihon Kēzai Shinbusha, 1981).

1900, but by 1928 CEO ownership had declined to less than 20 percent, and by 1962 it had fallen to less than 10 percent.[2] In the postwar period, many of the hired CEOs rose up through the company's permanent employment system; these executives made up almost 50 percent of all CEOs. Thus between 1900 and 1962, the position of the owner CEO and the hired CEO had reversed.

During the early Showa period, the massive conglomerates that were formed by the *zaibatsu* solidified their organizations and conservatively developed their businesses. However, as the Great Depression hit Japan and the world economy, farm villages withered, economic stagnation increased, and strong social opposition grew against the conservative *zaibatsu*. The progressive bureaucrats, the military, and the media fanned the flames of public opinion, criticized the dollar-buying speculation of Mitsui Bank and the Mitsui Trading Company during 1930–31 (which was actually a currency hedge against Britain going off the gold standard), and intensified pressure on the *zaibatsu*. The assassination of the Mitsui chairman, Takuma Dan, by rightists in March 1932 was symbolic of this growing public opinion.

In response to increasingly hostile public opinion, the *zaibatsu* went through a bold transformation to change some of their characteristics. Mitsui, which was under intense public attack, appointed Shigeaki Ikeda as its chairman and immediately began implementing policies designed to respond to unfavorable public opinion. He divested affiliated Mitsui companies and took the company public, strategies that weakened the power of the *zaibatsu* family and strengthened the authority of professional CEOs. Mitsui also joined with the military and the progressive bureaucrats to pursue economic order and industrialization.

Ironically, in later years the Allied Occupation saw the military and the *zaibatsu* as one entity and, for this very reason, pushed for the disbanding of the *zaibatsu*. However, the cooperation between the old *zaibatsu* and the military did not come from within but rather was the result of the "transformation" in response to public opinion and terrorism. The transformation of the *zaibatsu* was the result not only of public pressure but also of rapid change in the economic structure that stemmed from changes in government policy. In an aggressive response to the long depression and social instability created by frequent farmers' riots, the government advanced the

2. Yoshimatsu Aonuma, *Nihon no Kēē Sō* (Tokyo: Nikkēshinsho, 1965).

Takahashi Finance Plan, which rapidly increased regional and farm village public works projects in the form of temporary emergency works, increased the size of government across the board, including large increases in military and other public expenditures, and lowered the interest rate.[3]

The effects of this sudden ballooning of the military budget were widespread. First, it made possible the high-speed development of heavy industries. Second, many of the archetypes of the relationship between the government and the private sector were formed at this time, such as the cooperation between the government and the *zaibatsu* that had undergone transformation, the development of new technologies and new corporations centered on military needs, the regulation of financial policy, and the passage of corporate laws such as the Oil Industry Law. These developments, combined with the formation of the professional CEO system and the establishment of employee rights within the company that came about as a result of slow disbanding of the *zaibatsu,* gradually created the large private sector that was to become the backbone of postwar high growth. This wartime system was characterized by military priority and bureaucratic control, and demonstrated the strong influence of the government over the large private sector. Although the unusual environment of the war period and anti-*zaibatsu* public opinion were likely the main reasons for this influence, it was also related to the *zaibatsu* adapting to their environment and choosing to work with the military and the progressive bureaucrats. That this was the choice of the *zaibatsu* is clear because the relative

3. Takafusa Nakamura summarized the plan in the following manner:

> Takahashi, in 1920, instinctively knew the most important part of Keynes' general theory. The content of Takahashi's policies can be summarized as follows. First, the currency rate was allowed to depreciate temporarily. As a result, the Japan-U.S. exchange rate went from \$45/¥100 in 1931 to just below \$20/¥100 in 1932 and settled around \$30/¥100 (against 1 pound 2 shillings) in 1933. This was a 40 percent drop in the rate. It goes without saying that this had an effect on exports. Second was the bold domestic move to cut the interest rate. The Bank of Japan commercial acceptance rate (the discount rate), which was at its peak of 5.84 percent in 1931, fell to 3.56 percent in 1933. Third was an increase in government expenditure, which rose to 22.6 million yen in 1933. At the center of the increase in overall expenditure was an increase in the military budget (4.5 million yen in 1931, 6.9 million yen in 1932, and 8.7 million yen in 1933), a temporary emergency expenditure, and the farm village development expenditure (1.8 million yen in 1932, 2.1 million yen in 1933, and 1.6 million yen in 1934). Public bonds were underwritten by the Bank of Japan to make up for the lack of funds.

Takafusa Nakamura, *Nihon Kēzai—sono sēchō to kōzo* (Tokyo: Tokyo Daigaku Shuppankai, 1978), pp. 125, 116–17 (my translation).

power of the CEOs and the *zaibatsu* family was not that weak, despite the anti-*zaibatsu* public opinion.

In order to implement Kanji Ishiwara's "Five-Year Plan for Important Industries," and in the spirit of harmony, Senjurō Hayashi, who led the army, was made prime minister in 1937; Toyotarō Yūki from the financial sector was made minister of finance; and Shigeaki Ikeda was made the governor of the Bank of Japan.[4] Ikeda, who was targeted by the rightists along with Takuma Dan, took up the reform of the Mitsui *zaibatsu* and cooperated with the military because he saw it as a way to save Mitsui in the context of this harmony.[5]

Rapid Rise of the New *Zaibatsu*

The rise of the new *zaibatsu* was one of the noteworthy aspects of the 1930s and early 1940s that laid the foundation for postwar *keiretsu*. Hidemasa Morikawa points out that these new corporate groups were not *zaibatsu* by strict definition.[6] First, the percentage of cross-stockholding was low (even in Nissan, which was most like a *zaibatsu*): in 1937, there were only 5 percent cross-stockholdings between Nissan founder Yoshisuke Ayukawa and the rest of the group. Second, most of them had engineers as corporate leaders and were passionate about technological innovation. Third, many of them worked with the military and the progressive bureaucrats, who were opposed to, and functioned as a countervailing power to, the old *zaibatsu*. Men such as Satoru Mori of Showa Electric and Chikuhei Nakajima of Nakajima Aircraft were themselves politicians and were in a position to fully use their connections with the military and the bureaucracy. The greatest weakness of the new, compared to the old, *zaibatsu* was that they did not have their own financial institutions, which meant they

---

4. The "Five-Year Plan for Important Industries," drawn up in 1937, established specific production targets for certain products, including automobiles, machines, steel, oil, coal, aluminum, ships, and others, to be achieved within five years through the application of government control. The plan was developed by Kanji Ishiwara, a radical in the Japanese army who was instrumental in increasing government control of the economy.

5. Yukio Noguchi and I have called this wartime system the "total war economic system" and Noguchi has gone on to propose that it was the "1940s regime" and critically analyzed it as such. The Japanese capitalist system that was created during the period from the end of Taisho to the Showa period had wartime characteristics and its origins were certainly in the 1930s and 1940s. Eisuke Sakakibara and Yukio Noguchi, "Ōkurashō, Nichigin Ōchō no Bunseki—Sōryokusen Kēzai Taisē no Shūen," *Chuōkōron* (August 1977); Yukio Noguchi, *1940 nen Taisē* (Tokyo: Tōyō Kēzai Shinpōsha, 1995).

6. Morikawa, *Nihon Zaibatsu Shi*, p. 211 (my translation).

lacked financial power. Special banks, particularly the Industrial Bank of Japan (IBJ), supported them indirectly, and the government supported the role of the IBJ.[7]

To respond to the immense demand for capital, mainly from the new *zaibatsu*, loan syndicates were formed for the frequent injection of capital, with IBJ as the lead manager. From 1939 to 1941, there were 176 such loan syndicates, in 118 of which IBJ took the lead. Riken Science Industries, Nakajima Aircraft, Toyota Motors, Nissan Motors, and Hitachi Manufacturing were the main recipients of the funds. It was at this time that the foundation for the postwar financial system was laid with the rapid concentration of the old *zaibatsu* banks, the quick expansion of postal and agricultural cooperatives (with their Savings Department later becoming the Trust Fund Bureau), and the centering of the capital supply method in the IBJ. In addition, in 1942 the Bank of Japan Act, which was to become the legal foundation of postwar financial policy, was enacted.

Many of the new *zaibatsu* had their foundations in the colonies, which led to their postwar disbanding; however, companies such as Toyota, Nissan, Hitachi, and Toshiba, which would lead the high-growth period, also came out of this group, and the engineering prowess of others such as Riken Science Industries and Nakajima Aircraft, which were disbanded after the war, became an important source of postwar engineering innovation. In addition to this specific legacy, the postwar influence of the new *zaibatsu* was momentous because it gave birth to a corporate culture that had technology at its core. Takafusa Nakamura states that the "way of the new *zaibatsu* was similar to the way postwar Sony, National, Sanyo, Sharp, and more recently Pioneer used their engineering as a weapon in their sudden rise."[8]

Also important to the postwar economic system were the corporate laws, enacted in quick succession around 1935. Typical of these was the Oil Industry Law of 1934. At the time, oil was imported and then refined

7. In 1937, under the Temporary Capital Adjustment Law, issuance of bank debentures by IBJ was increased from ¥500 million to ¥1 billion, and the Gold Asset Special Account underwrote ¥300 million of that. In addition, the Deposit Department (currently the Trust Fund Bureau) and the Bank of Japan supplied money to IBJ through short-term loans and rediscounts. As a result, IBJ's loan balance, which was ¥380 million from April to October 1936, became ¥1.16 billion by the end of 1937, experiencing a threefold increase in almost two years. The amount of loans continued to increase beyond 1938 with the support of the government and, under the Temporary Capital Adjustment Law, the bank debenture issue increased to ¥10 billion in 1945.

8. Takatusa Nakamura, *Shōwa Kēzai Shi,* Iwanami Seminar Book 17 (Tokyo: Iwanami Shoten, 1986), p. 92 (my translation).

to produce gasoline and heavy oil. The aim of the legislation was to control and specially protect the resource because of its importance to the military. After the Oil Industry Law, legislation such as the Automobile Manufacturing Industry Law and Steel Industry Law of 1936 and the Machine Tool Industry Law and the Aircraft Manufacturing Industry Law of 1938 were passed. It was during this time that the archetype of the postwar policymaking mechanism was created by organizing industries through industry laws, giving administrative guidance through the industrial associations, and incorporating the views of the industry in government policy.

Competition Guided by the Visible Hand

The Japanese corporate system, or Japanese management system, has been successful because of its corporate culture built around technology and the permanently employed professional management staff, which was influenced by humanism, permanent employment, seniority, and industry-specific associations. Although the Japanese system was different from the neoclassical model, it created an environment of continuous technological innovation and fierce competition. Indeed, one aspect of the Japanese system that was created from the prewar legacy of large export-oriented companies such as Toyota is the *keiretsu*, which is characterized by business transactions conducted within corporate groups. In current parlance, *keiretsu* could be referred to as an efficient B2B (business-to-business) system. In spite of criticisms of certain aspects of the *keiretsu* (for example, its dual system of wages and employment and its closed subcontracting relationships), there were many management reforms, such as the just-in-time system and designing-in, which the United States adopted from Japan during the 1980s and 1990s.

In comparison to the neoclassical competition of the invisible hand, Hiroyuki Itami characterized the B2B system of the *keiretsu* as competition guided by the "visible hand" and skillfully described its characteristics (see table 5-1).[9] Compared with market competition, the *keiretsu* system had certain shortcomings, such as the limited freedom allowed to individual companies, strong group management, and a tendency to become rigid over the medium to long term. On the other hand, the advantages of tech-

9. Hiroyuki Itami, *Kyōsō to Kakushin—Jidōsha Sangyō no Kigyō Sēchō* (Tokyo: Tōyō Kēzai Shinpōsha, 1998).

Table 5-1. *Keiretsu Competition by the "Visible Hand"
Compared with Market Competition*

Feature	Market competition	The visible hand
Number of transacting parties	Multiple and anonymous	Few Face-to-face management possible
Freedom of entry and exit	Freedom to "exit from transaction," but not necessarily from market	Very little Long-term, fixed relationships
Discipline mechanism	Exit from unsatisfactory transaction	Threat of potential exit Expression of dissatisfaction
Incentive to cooperate	None	Cooperation around technology accumulation; contributes to technological innovation
Transparency of information	Public information: does not incur observation cost No information gap among sellers: complete diffusion of productive technology information	Technology information gap Many types of buyer-seller information transactions: costs of observation and transmission incurred
Existence of controlling body	None ("invisible hand")	Parent company ("visible hand"): buyer has strong monopolistic power Base of control is information collection and its function as information center

Source: Compiled from Hiroyuki Itami, *Kyōsō to Kakushin—Jidōsha Sangyō no Kigyō Sēchō* (Tokyo: Tōyō Kēzai Shinpōsha, 1998), chap. 6 (my translation).

nology and information sharing were numerous. In current terms, the efficient manufacturing and supply of parts under the just-in-time system made possible by information sharing could be viewed as particularly effective supply chain management.

In addition, because of the mutual trust built up over the long term, *keiretsu* companies shared technology that allowed them to develop products and efficiently pursue innovation. Technology sharing was largely possible in part because inter-*keiretsu* and interpersonal relationships were at

Table 5-2. Keiretsu Relationships[a]

Company	Largest stockholders (percentage ownership)	Seconded personnel	Isuzu	Honda	Fuji	Mazda	Daihatsu	Suzuki	Mitsubishi	Hino	Nissan	Toyota
Toyota Keiretsu												
Aishin Shōki	Toyota Motors (21.3); Toyota Jidō Shokki (5.6)	Director, auditor					•	•	•	•		•
Nihon Densō	Toyota Motors (21.2); Toyota Jidō Shokki (7)	Chairman, CEO, senior managing directors (senmu) 2, managing directors (jōmu) 4, directors 2, auditor	•	•	•	•		•	•			•
Toyota Gōsē	Toyota Motors (46.8); Toyota Tsūshō (1.8); Nihon Densō (1.4)	CEO, senior managing director, managing directors 2, auditor	•	•	•		•	•	•	•		•
Aisan Kōgyō	Toyota Motors (24.3); Toyota Jidō Shokki (22.2)	CEO, managing directors 2, director, auditor	•	•		•	•		•			•
Nissan Keiretsu												
Atsugi Jidōshabuhin	Nissan Motors (40.4); Nissan Tochi Tatemono (3.4); Nissan Diesel (2.4)	Chairman, CEO, managing directors 4, directors 4, auditors 4				•					•	
Nihon Radiator	Nissan Motors (40.8)	Chairman, CEO, managing directors 3, director, auditor			•	•					•	
Kokusan Kinzoku Kōgyō	Nissan Motors (25.0)		•		•				•		•	
Hashimoto Forming Kōgyō	Nissan Motors (34.8)	Managing director, directors 3, auditor	•	•	•						•	

Source: Itami, *Kyōsō to Kakushin*, p. 168 (my translation).
a. Data for Toyota are from 1984; data for Nissan, from 1985.

the core of the Japanese system, an asset that cannot be implemented in an open system like the Internet. Another factor that favored competition by the "visible hand" was that the *keiretsu* was not a completely closed system. Table 5-2 was compiled from previously cited sources, such as Hiroyuki Itami, that revealed the situation in the mid-1980s, when Japanese companies were at their peak in the international market. For example, Nihon Densō, which is a member of the Toyota *keiretsu*, supplied parts to six other automobile manufacturers besides Toyota. However, table 5-2 also shows that Toyota *keiretsu* companies did not supply parts to Nissan and Nissan *keiretsu* companies did not supply parts to Toyota.

Although many Japanese-style large export-oriented companies grew in competition with those from the West while simultaneously creating Japanese B2B relationships like those in the *keiretsu* system, the development of the information technology (IT) revolution created a new wave of globalization and brought many of the problems of the Japanese system to the surface.

In order to help Nissan break through the current Japanese stagnation, Carlos Ghosn implemented revolutionary and fundamental reforms.[10] First was the introduction of a new merit-based system. During the three months before his appointment as chief operating officer (COO), he individually met with approximately 600 mid-level employees, and many who were thought to have special ability were appointed to mid-level management positions. Although the rigid seniority system was dismantled, it is interesting that most employees were still promoted through internal advancement (except for the subordinates that he brought over from Renault). The Japanese permanent employment system was not completely rejected, but Ghosn understood it is important to motivate talented employees in an organization.

The second of Ghosn's reforms was referred to as the "horizontal revolution," which was a rejection of the vertically divided organization. He created nine cross-functional teams and used them to form a comprehensive strategic management system. In recognizing that vertical sectionalism is somewhat of a pitfall for Japanese organizations, this "horizontal revolution" could be useful for many organizations.

His third reform was dismantling the *keiretsu*. Although the mergers of *keiretsu* companies and the reduction in the number of subcontractors had

---

10. Yōzō Hasegawa, *Ghosn-san no Shita de Hatarakitai Desu ka* (Tokyo: Nikkei Business Bunko, 2001).

strong elements of cultural revolution, this action did not constitute a complete tearing down of the *keiretsu* system. Rather, it was an effort to introduce new supply chain management through revitalization. It was a revolution to reduce costs and increase the efficiency of the supply process through the reorganization of steel companies and the restructuring of parts and raw material makers.

The fourth reform was the globalization of management and personnel. This probably was easier for Ghosn to implement because he himself was a non-Japanese COO. Such a revolution should have come much earlier, particularly for large Japanese export-oriented companies that were dramatically behind in the globalization of their personnel.

Ongoing Corporate Revolution

While the "Ghosn Revolution" was notable in the sense that a non-Japanese COO implemented changes, with some immediate success, the same revolution is proceeding to different degrees in many of the large export-oriented corporations. In particular, the attempts to increase efficiency in manufacturing and sales through information technology and to develop new businesses are reforms that many companies have undertaken. For example, Toyota Motors is using information technology in its automobile manufacturing and is expanding business into many other IT-related areas: it is expanding into Internet communications through KDDI, creating a cable television and cellular business, and moving into financial services such as insurance and investment banking.

Change is occurring even for the *shōsha*, the B2B trading companies that are very "Japanese" and have no parallels anywhere in the world. In the context of declining handling fees and the changes in the Japanese *keiretsu*, the *shōsha*, which typically have a vertical structure, are utilizing new information technology and undergoing horizontal reform. For example, the Mitsubishi Corporation has created, directly under the president, a New Business Initiative Group that will interact with the six preexisting business groups. By creating a horizontal axis to cut through the vertical corporate structure, the company is trying to strategically revive and strengthen the general trading company's functions by maximizing know-how accumulated in the "real world" to establish new business models which generate synergy when combined with the expanding on-line world.

What is of interest here is that, like Toyota Motors, Mitsubishi Corporation is expanding into broader B2C (business-to-consumer) businesses in areas such as finance and distribution with the help of information technology. Currently, the company owns the Lawson and Kentucky Fried Chicken franchises. Further expansion under way may include the possibility of entering the medical industry.

As can be seen from the two examples of Toyota Motors and Mitsubishi Corporation, external factors such as the current developments in information technology and renewed globalization are having a large impact. What the two companies have in common is that, while maintaining the preexisting B2B relationships that are typical of *keiretsu*, they are also attempting to revitalize their operations by trying to incorporate information technology and form new horizontal groups to create a new organization. In other words, while maintaining their preexisting core competencies in automobile manufacturing and B2B commerce, respectively, they are also using information technology to look for new business opportunities in many fields that are related to these core competencies.

This trend is not a choice between old business and new business or between "bricks and mortar" and information technology; neither is it Japanese versus Anglo-Saxon management. It is progress based on response to the company's business environment and the dynamic evolution of the preexisting system, which is constantly changing shape and surviving in new ways. The Japanese company, which has been gradually forming since the 1930s, is experiencing the end of modernization and industrialization and is seeking a new transformation in the age of globalization and information. However, this new transformation is neither Americanization nor the surrender to a global standard; rather, it is the process of creating a new kind of Japanese company.

6 The Japanese Banking System and Its Nonperforming Loan Problem

In a market economy, a bubble can develop, and when it bursts, it can cause balance sheet problems, or worse, a crisis of the entire financial system. Both the United States and Western Europe suffered these effects from the latter half of the 1980s through the 1990s. However, compared with Japan, the duration of the economic crisis was relatively short. By the mid-1990s balance sheet problems had been resolved and the financial instability had ended. At issue is why Japan has suffered from the effects of the burst longer than the United States and Western Europe.

One reason could be poor fiscal, monetary, or financial supervisory policies. Yet the failure of macroeconomic and supervisory policies does not provide a thorough explanation for why Japan's recession has lasted so long. Compared with many developing countries in Asia and Latin America, Japanese policies were far better, and were certainly no worse than policies implemented in other developed countries.

However, if the focus shifts from the macroeconomic to the microeconomic, and from GDP analysis to structural analysis, a different picture emerges. When structural reform is mentioned, non-Japanese investors immediately point to the need to resolve the nonperforming loan (NPL) problem.

The current total of nonperforming loans depends on how NPLs are defined. The three basic methods for classifying NPLs in Japan are the risk-managed credit method, the internal assessment method, and the method based on the Finance Revitalization Act.[1] Depending upon which classification is used, the total amount of Japan's NPLs is between ¥31.8 and ¥63.9 trillion.[2] Table 6-1 shows the characteristics of each classification method.

Yet more problematic than the absolute amount of current NPLs is that this amount has not declined, in spite of the injection of public funds and banks' actions to absorb large NPL losses. The number of debtors in the Classification II category is actually increasing. From 1992 to mid-2000, the national bank cumulative total of NPLs that had been absorbed had grown to ¥68 trillion. In the second half of 2000, Japan's sixteen major banks had absorbed an additional ¥4.4 trillion. Figure 6-1 illustrates the amount of losses due to settlement of nonperforming loans.

The reason the amount of NPLs has not declined is that debtors in the domestic manufacturing and service industries have not pursued structural reform. Whereas the reorganization of financial institutions is already in progress, and the export-related manufacturing sector (including the automobile industry) has for the most part improved its cost structure and profitability, the construction and distribution industries have not undergone organizational or structural reform. Without the reform and reorganization of these industries, the problem of NPLs cannot be resolved.

Thus the reason Japan has endured a longer period of financial instability compared with the United States and Western Europe is a lack of microeconomic structural reform. Without revitalization of the domestic manufacturing and service industries, which are not internationally competitive and have low productivity, it will be extremely difficult to overcome the

1. In addition, the Democratic Party proposed another formulation that identifies "problem assets" as the total of bankrupt debtors, effectively bankrupt debtors, and debtors in danger of bankruptcy. The Financial Supervisory Agency tallied these; they totaled ¥111 trillion as of September 2000. This sum is large because it includes assets that banks have already dealt with through provisioning or securing with solid collateral. Not all of those assets should be categorized as nonperforming loans. The difference between the ¥111 trillion and the ¥63.9 trillion determined by the internal assessment method is ¥47.1 trillion, which would be Classification II (in danger of bankruptcy) debt.

2. As of the account settlement date in September 2000, the national bank total of NPLs was ¥31.8 trillion according to the risk-managed credit method, ¥63.9 trillion according to the internal assessment method, and ¥32.9 trillion according to the criteria in the Finance Revitalization Act.

Table 6-1. *Methods of Classifying Nonperforming Loans*

Characteristics	Risk-managed credit	Internal assessment	Finance Revitalization Act
Basic law	The Banking Act and Bank Operation Rules	Guidelines for banks' disclosure of their NPLs	Finance Revitalization Act
Date of implementation	Since March 1993: disclosure based on uniform standard was required as of March 1998	Since March 1998	Since March 1999 for main banks, since Sept. 1999 for other banks, since March 2000 for cooperative associations
Objective	Disclosure	For the calculation of loan loss reserves	Disclosure
Relevant assets	Loans	Total assets (however, aggregate results announced by the authorities are based on total credits, including off-balance-sheet items)	Total credits (debt securities, loans, foreign exchange, uncollected interest, temporary disbursements, guarantees)
Classification method	Classification based on objective criteria for individual credit assessment (except for some financial institutions where classification is based on assessment of debtor's financial condition). Categories are: Failed credit / Credit in arrears / Credit more than 3 months in arrears / Credit for which loan conditions eased	Classification based on debtor's financial condition as: Bankrupt / Effectively bankrupt / In danger of bankruptcy / Needs attention / Normal. Classification after realistic determination of collection probability based on collateral and loan loss reserves. I–IV classifications (the higher the number, the worse the situation); II and higher are considered classified assets	Classification based on debtor's financial condition, rather than based solely on objective criteria for assessment of individual credit. Categories are: Bankruptcy-rehabilitated credit / Credit at risk / Credit needs attention / Normal credit
Handling of collateral and reserves	Collateral and loan loss reserves are deducted from face amount of credit	Classification is based on coverage of collateral; individual reserves, good quality collateral and guarantees are assigned a classification of I	Collateral and loan loss reserves are deducted from face amount of credit

Source: Sanwa Sōgō Kenkyūjyo, *Furyōsaiken Mondai no Genjyo* (Tokyo: May 2001), p. 2.

Figure 6-1. *Cumulative National Bank Settlement Loss
from Nonperforming Loans*[a]

Trillions of yen

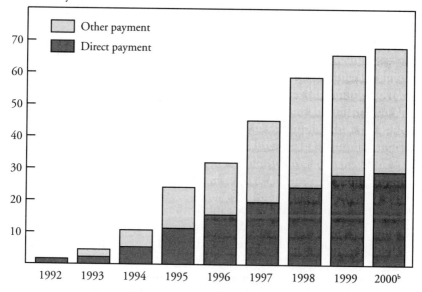

Source: Financial Services Agency, *Risk Kanri Saikennado no Jyōkyō*. Reproduced in *Furyōsaiken Mondai no Genjyō* (Sanwa Sōgō Kenkyujyo, May 29, 2001), p. 3.

a. Direct payment includes loan repayment, seller loss in joint credit takeover, and support loss. Other payment includes reserves to cover bad debt. Data are for the fiscal year, running from April 1 of the given year to March 31 of the next.

b. Interim fiscal year, ending September 30, 2000.

current long-term structural recession or the problem of NPLs. It is imperative that these sectors undergo structural and systemic reform.

As mentioned in chapter 4, the main obstacle to reform for the low-productivity sectors of domestic manufacturing and service industries is Japan's economic and political dual structure. Several steps are necessary to reform this structure, including revision of domestic laws and ordinances, reallocation of budget resources, and changes in political and administrative procedures. This chapter discusses the structural reform of the banking system.[3]

3. This is a key reform because the reorganization of the main banking system at the end of the 1990s and the dramatic decline in the contingency governance ability of banks are two major reasons why the nonperforming loan problem has been prolonged. In the past banks were deeply involved with

Resolving the Lingering Nonperforming Loan Problem

Paul Sheard characterizes what has been called "Japanese capitalism" as "main bank capitalism," because main banks are an important part of the Japanese corporate governance function:

> In the Japanese (insider-based) corporate governance system, the function of monitoring and intervention, which is the central function of governance, is characterized by "concentration" and the "division of labor." . . . "Concentration" does not mean that all of the investor clients who participate in the capital market are directly or aggressively involved in monitoring and intervention; it refers to a specific investor who concentrates on monitoring and intervention. If monitoring and intervention is "concentrated," even if there are a hundred investors, one of them, the main bank, concentrates on monitoring and intervention; the resulting benefit also goes to the other ninety-nine investors. In this sense, it can be said the concentrated monitoring and intervention function is somewhat like a local public good. . . . [T]he "division of labor" is a characteristic that has not been described until now. It means that the monitoring and intervention is concentrated, sometimes with the main bank and at other times with the parent company, and refers to the division of labor of the monitoring and intervention function between main banks and parent companies. . . .
>
> Because until now only the monitoring function "concentrated" in the main banks was emphasized, the monitoring function of the parent companies had been neglected. However, if we look at the actuality in Japan, the main banks are not monitoring all of the publicly traded parent companies. In fact, the large publicly traded companies are also monitoring and intervening in their publicly traded subsidiaries. With regard to the Japanese governance system, it is correct to think of the main banks and parent companies as having the primary role in monitoring.[4]

---

the governance of domestic companies and, depending on the situation, were also involved in the structural reform of those companies. There are several well-known examples, such as the reorganization of Asahi Beer by Sumitomo Bank and the reform of Hitachi Shipbuilding by Sanwa Bank. This is what some have called "contingency governance" by main banks.

4. Paul Sheard, *Mein Banku Shihon Shugi no Kiki* (Tokyo: Tōyō Kēzai Shinpōsha, 1997), pp. 117–18 (my translation).

Among the banks that finance a company, the main bank has a long and continuous business relationship with the company, as it finances a substantial share of the company and has the responsibility of supervising it. Normally, in addition to financing, main banks hold the stocks, send directors, settle accounts, and hold the corporate bonds. Main banks disseminate management information, provide foreign currency, issue securities, and give advice on issues such as mergers and acquisitions. Although the main bank does not exclusively finance client companies (it is normal for other banks to finance the company as well), it is usually the lead manager in loan syndicates.[5]

When indirect financing plays a greater role than direct financing, it is natural to have main bank–centered corporate governance. This is the case not only in Japan but also in developed capitalist markets generally. For example, Germany's Hausbank, which monitors and intervenes, is the lead bank and as such has an important function. By contrast, when companies raise money from external sources such as stocks and bonds, as is the case in the United States and Great Britain, the stockholders conduct corporate governance.

In Japan before the 1930s, these characteristics of the main bank system did not exist. Instead, companies used internal capital accumulation, as well as stock and bonds, to raise capital. The Meiji period (1868–1912) was a time of internal financing in which companies largely depended upon stocks and internal capital accumulation. The *zaibatsu* wielded a lot of power through monopolistic control of their extremely profitable mines and export businesses, and through their strong relationship with the government. As a result, they were able to expand their businesses by internal accumulation and reinvestment. Although companies issued stocks, they were owned by a small number of wealthy *zaibatsu* families and landowners; almost 90 percent of bank loans went to these wealthy families with stocks as collateral.

After World War I, the rise of heavy industry (1914–30) made it difficult to raise enough capital through internal accumulation, and external sourcing of capital began to increase rapidly. Companies raised funds from many external stockholders, and it became common practice for companies to borrow from banks. As illustrated in figure 6-2, the share of bank loans at this time had settled around 20 percent, while stocks and internal

---

5. Masahiko Aoki and Hugh Patrick, eds., *The Japanese Main Bank System: Its Relevance for Developing and Transforming Economies* (Oxford University Press, 1994).

Figure 6-2. *Capital Sourcing by Large Corporations,*
Taisho and Early Showa Periods

Percent

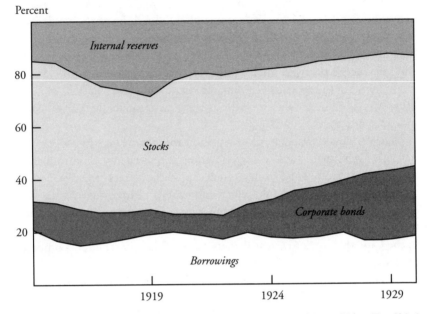

Source: Masahiko Aoki and Hugh Patrick, eds., *The Japanese Main Bank System* (Tokyo: Tōyō Keizai Shinpōsha, 1996), p. 72 (my translation).

reserves totaled more than 50 percent. Capital accumulation through corporate bonds had increased as the proportion of internal funds had decreased.

However, in 1927, Japan encountered its worst economic crisis ever. As a result, banks were reorganized and merged, and the government pursued stronger regulation of the financial system. Table 6-2 shows the financial regulations enacted after 1927. The foundation of the main bank system as it is today developed during this process of increased regulation.

The promotion of loan syndication for long-term investment, which began in the 1930s, and the establishment of the special military supply financing system in 1944 were particularly significant for the development of the main bank system. The Ministry of Munitions was involved in securing financing and planning the production of military supplies. As companies received orders for military provisions, they were also assigned a bank, which supplied capital necessary for production. At the end of the

Table 6-2. *Finance Regulation Enacted, 1927–49*

Year	Regulation	Characteristics of regulation
1927	Banking Act	Promote consolidation of banks; strengthen administrative guidance authority
1937	Temporary Capital Sourcing Act	Allot capital to equip priority military supply industries
1940	Order for lending by banks and other institutions	Drive capital allotment for priority military supply industries
1941	Key Industry Control Order[a]	Control organizations were set up for each industry to implement economic planning
1942	Finance Control Organization Order	Control of financial institutions by the national finance control organizations
1943	Military Supply Corporation Act[a]	Direct control of production by the government
1944	Designated Financial Institution System	Assign main bank to each military supply corporation
1947	Mediation by the Bank of Japan Bond Issuance Coordination Committee	Drive capital adjustment of large corporations; bond issuance adjustment, standardization of issuance conditions
1948	Temporary Interest Adjustment Act	Interest rate control over loans and deposits
1949	Foreign Exchange Control Act	Interception of internal and external finance

Source: Tetsuji Okazaki and Masahiro Okano, *Gendai Nihon Keizai Shisutemu no Genryū* (Tokyo: Nihon Keizai Shinbunsha, 1993), p. 37.

a. Not directly a finance-related regulation.

war, the assigned-bank system applied to 2,240 companies; of those, 1,582 companies were assigned to one of the five large *zaibatsu* banks.

During this time, the Industrial Bank of Japan increased financial assets using postal savings, and by doing so injected capital into industrial development. The rationalization, bank mergers, concentrated investment, and bank assignments, along with the rise of the Industrial Bank of Japan to the position of Japan's national policymaking bank, became the foundation of the post–World War II main bank system.

During the early postwar reforms, the government (through the Holding Company Liquidation Commission, HCLC, which comprised Japanese bureaucrats working in conjunction with occupation authorities) dissolved the *zaibatsu* and abolished holding companies. Under farmland reform, *zaibatsu* families lost their lands to farmers. As a result, the Japanese capitalist class was largely devastated. Although at first it seemed that the General Headquarters (GHQ), the Allies' executive authority, was thinking of radical financial system reform, as the Cold War structure became established, the influence of reformists such as C. Keddies of the Civil Administration Department weakened, and thus the fundamental structure of the financial system remained intact. The government's regulation of finance continued in almost the same way. Bank possession of nonfinancial company stocks also continued, although it was initially limited to 5 percent. This bank ownership of stock maintained and revived the old *zaibatsu* company relationships based on the cross holding of stocks and became a part of the postwar main bank–centered *keiretsu* system.

The government (in conjunction with the occupation authority, under which the Japanese gained more and more control as years passed) implemented several financial reforms, including the separation of the banking business from the securities business (in a law similar to the Glass-Steagall Act in the United States) and the privatization of the government-controlled long-term credit and foreign-exchange banks. However, for several decades after World War II, the main function of private banks (complemented by government-affiliated banks) was to supply long-term funds to private sector companies and, as such, the banking system did not need to fundamentally change.

As part of the effort to make securities public, the Securities Adjustment Cooperative Committee sold shares worth ¥25.2 billion in July 1947 (approximately 57 percent of total corporate investment capital at the end of 1945). Half of the securities sold were those bought from *zaibatsu* families and holding companies or were government-held securities that were payment-in-kind from *zaibatsu* families. The objective was to sell these assets at a specified price to regular households. As a result, the share of stocks held by individuals increased from 51.9 percent in 1945 to 61.9 percent in 1949, and the share held by corporations fell from 24.6 percent to 5.6 percent.

At the same time, the issuance of new stocks to help corporations rebuild led to a fall in the value of stocks in the summer of 1945, which developed into a deep securities depression. This led to private individuals selling off the newly acquired stocks, which caused the share of the market held by individuals to decline to 57 percent in 1951. The confusion that ensued over corporate control pushed companies to hold each other's stocks, a move that became one of the primary factors for the establishment of the postwar main bank system.

During the high-growth period of the early 1950s to the mid-1970s, the main bank system was at its peak as the rapid growth of business led to a shortage of investment capital. In addition, financial markets were regulated and underdeveloped, and maintaining a relationship with a main bank was the central pillar of the private sector's financial strategy. During the high-growth period, a stable system was created in which banks and other financial institutions could mobilize and distribute savings, and the government gently controlled financial markets, with the demand for capital outweighing the supply. New entrants into the banking industry were not approved and financial market activities were partitioned among the long-term credit banks, trust banks, city banks, and regional banks. With the involvement of the Bank of Japan, funds were selectively distributed to large borrowers. Although it was a "Japanese" system very different from the neoclassical model, it worked well during this period.

As noted previously, the confusion over the effort to increase private individuals' stockholdings and the accompanying upset of the corporate ownership relationship pushed management to cross hold stocks as a stabilization measure. In 1952, it became possible for former *zaibatsu* companies to regroup and for new financial groups to form, thus reviving the *zaibatsu*-style practice of cross holding stocks. In 1953, the limitation of 5 percent shareholding of corporations by financial institutions (stipulated by the 1947 Antitrust Law) was changed to 10 percent because of strong demands from organizations such as the Keidanren. As a result, the cross holding of stocks, with banks at the core, dramatically increased. This increased the autonomy of corporate management vis-à-vis stockholders and strengthened the control of banks, particularly main banks, over companies.

Following the 1973 oil shock, 1974 was Japan's first year of negative growth after the end of World War II. Companies tried to adjust to the slowdown in the economic growth rate through asset restructuring and debt reduction. Corporate investment also decreased, individual savings outweighed individual investment, and large companies reduced their dependency on bank loans. For export-oriented companies that were making gains in the perception of product reliability, the securities market was an effective source of external capital. Affected by deregulation and low interest rates, particularly toward the end of the 1980s, capital markets experienced a large influx of capital. It became very normal for companies to access capital though equity financing.

While decreasing the supply of loans to large, powerful companies and considering increasing securities-related and other investment services, banks shifted their lending from the manufacturing sector to the service sector and from large to medium and small companies and individuals. The increase in loans to these companies, secured mainly by collateral that does not necessarily have corporate governance capability (such as real estate), has become a major cause of the nonperforming loan problem since the 1990s.

Table 6-3 shows the breakdown of external capital flows of nonfinancial companies from the 1930s to the 1990s. Private sector financial institution loans increased from the 1930s, peaked at the end of the 1960s, and began to decline rapidly thereafter. Figures 6-3 and 6-4, respectively, show the national bank loan recipient shares by sector and the tertiary sector loan shares by industry from 1965 to 2000. The manufacturing sector's share decreased from 48 percent to 15 percent in thirty-five years, and the current share of loans to the tertiary sector and individuals is 82 percent of total loans. Within the tertiary sector, loans to the real estate, financial services, insurance, and service industries have greatly increased. In 2000, if the construction industry is included, the share amounted to two-thirds of total tertiary loans.

With this process of structural change in the credit area, banks' ability to monitor companies greatly declined. The private sector moved away from the watchfulness of banks as it became less dependent upon bank loans in favor of other types of financing (such as stocks) while maintaining overall independence from stockholders. In turn, many banks that did not have the expertise to monitor tertiary industries or individuals became dependent on collateral, such as real estate and stocks. Consequently, banks' ability to monitor this sector did not improve.

Unfortunately for Japanese companies, the weakening of the main bank system and the deterioration of management discipline happened at the same time the Japanese economy matured and opportunities for low-risk investments decreased. Ordinarily under these circumstances, companies and lenders should conduct risk evaluation rigorously and execute corporate activities with the full understanding of risk and return. However, many companies and lending banks neglected to do this. Instead, they invested in areas that did not necessarily produce medium- or long-range returns, such as golf courses and resorts.

Table 6-3. *External Capital Flows of Nonfinancial Companies, Five-Year Averages*

Percent of total external capital flows

Period	Stocks	Bonds	Private sector financial institutions	Other
Concentrated bank system				
1936–40	43	7	50	1
1941–45	17	6	75	2
1946–50	13	4	72	11
Main bank system peak				
1951–55	14	4	72	10
1956–60	14	5	73	8
1961–65	16	4	73	7
1966–70	7	3	81	9
1971–75	6	5	78	11
Market-focused main bank system				
1976–80	8	6	72	14
1981–85	8	8	77	7
1986–90	10	13	59	19
1991–95	4	21	43	32

Source: Aoki and Patrick, *The Japanese Main Bank System*, p. 72; Okazaki and Okano, *Gendai Nihon Keizai Shisutemu no Genrū*, p. 37. Data before 1970 are from Bank of Japan (BOJ), *Sangyo Shikin Kyokyu Jokyo* (Tokyo, various issues); data after 1970, from BOJ, *Shikin Jyunkan Kanjo* (Tokyo, various issues).

Formation and Transformation of Main Bank Capitalism

Over the last ten years, the system of cross holding stocks among and between companies and banks, which was at the core of the main bank system, has gradually changed. Figure 6-5 shows the change in the share distribution of listed securities over the last ten years. The percentage of stable shareholdings declined from 46 percent in 1987 to 38 percent in 1999. Stable shareholdings here include the cross holding of stocks, stocks held by financial institutions, stocks of financial institutions held by companies, and stocks of related companies. The increase in the share of stocks held by foreigners in the 1990s is significant and that share has continued to grow.

Figure 6-6 shows the rates of cross shareholdings in the market as a whole and the shift in cross shareholdings of banks and companies. During

Figure 6-3. *Bank Loan Recipients*[a]

Percent

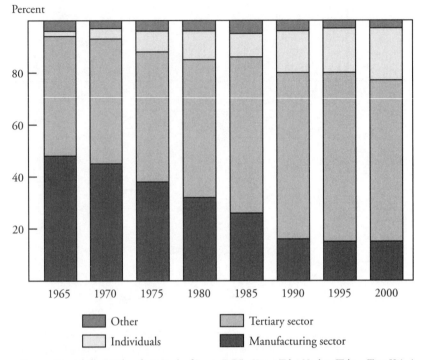

Other   Tertiary sector

Individuals   Manufacturing sector

Source: Compiled using data from Bank of Japan (BOJ), *Keizai Tōkei Nenkan* (Tokyo: Tōyō Keizai Shinpōsha, various issues); BOJ, *Keizai Tōkei Nenpo* (Tokyo: Nihon Ginko Chosa Tōkei Kyoku, various issues); and BOJ, *Kinyu Keizai Tōkei Geppo* (Tokyo: Nihon Ginko Chosa Tōkei Kyoku, various issues).

a. Data until 1993 are for banks nationwide; data after 1993 are for domestic banks.

the past ten years, cross shareholdings have decreased by almost half, down to 10 percent. In particular, bank stocks held by companies have fallen to less than 2 percent.

The change in the main bank system in terms of the cross holding of stocks and the shift toward foreign investors in the distribution of shareholdings demonstrate the increasing power that investment trusts, pension funds, other institutional investors, and individuals have on corporate governance through the stock market. Does this augur the breakdown of the main bank system and will it completely transform into the Anglo-Saxon system? Although there is a definite acceleration and convergence toward

Figure 6-4. *Loans to the Tertiary Sector, by Industry*

Percent

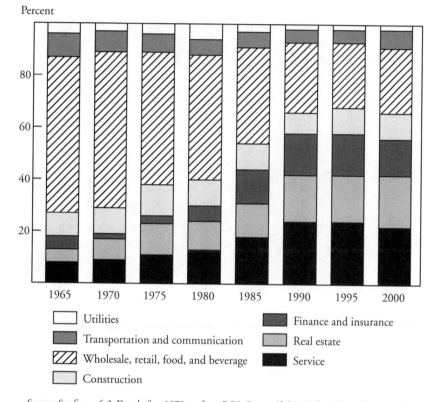

1965   1970   1975   1980   1985   1990   1995   2000

☐ Utilities   ■ Finance and insurance

■ Transportation and communication   ☐ Real estate

▨ Wholesale, retail, food, and beverage   ■ Service

☐ Construction

Source: See figure 6-3. Data before 1970 are from BOJ, *Sangyo Shikin Kyokyu Jokyo*; after 1970, from BOJ, *Shikin Jyunkan Kantei.*

market governance, neither the main banks nor the Japanese system will completely disappear.

Table 6-4 shows the results of questionnaires given to main banks in 1999. Many companies continue to obtain financing through main banks. Even though the sources of financing are becoming more diverse and the monitoring by stockholders through the stock market is strengthening, lending and monitoring by main banks will continue. For the main banks to revive their monitoring function in an effective way, they must quickly resolve the legacy of past monitoring failures and the NPL problem.

Figure 6-5. *Stockholder Structure for Listed Stocks*[a]

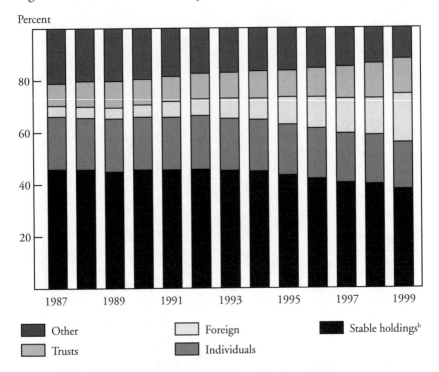

Percent

Source: "Kabushhiki Mochiai Jōkyō Chōsa" (NLI Research Institute, 1999).
a. Data are for end of year.
b. Stable stockholdings = cross-stockholdings + stocks held by financial institutions + financial institution stock held by companies + stock held by related companies.

Without clarifying their responsibility for past failures or resolving the negative outcome of that legacy, the banks will have difficulty reinvigorating themselves, let alone reviving their corporate monitoring function. If the government does not act positively to resolve the NPL problem, competitiveness will inevitably decline and the tertiary sector, particularly the heavily regulated and subsidized service industries of construction and real estate, will wither along with the banks.

The dissolution of the two dual structures mentioned in chapter 4 and the difficulty in resolving the NPL problem are deeply connected. If banks were to quickly resolve the NPL problem and create a new system of corporate governance that pushed out noncompetitive companies in the man-

Figure 6-6. *Composition of the Cross-Shareholding Ratio, Value Basis*[a]

Percent

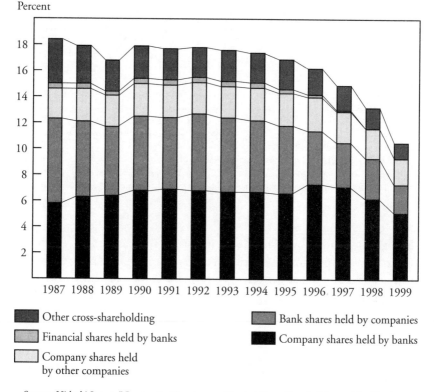

■ Other cross-shareholding   ▨ Bank shares held by companies

▨ Financial shares held by banks   ■ Company shares held by banks

☐ Company shares held
by other companies

Source: Hideaki Inoue, "Companies Continue to Unwind Cross-Shareholdings—The Fiscal 1999 Cross-Shareholding Survey," no. 145 (NLI Research Institute, 2000), p. 13; Fumiaki Kuroki, "The Present Status of Unwinding of Cross-Shareholding—The Fiscal 2000 Survey of Cross-Shareholding," no. 157 (NLI Research Institute, 2001), p. 29.

a. Data are for the fiscal year, running from April 1 of the given year to March 31 of the next.

ufacturing and service sectors, those industries could be revitalized. The government must deregulate policies intended to protect vested interests and decrease subsidies for those industries.

Only after the government makes progress in dissolving the system of protection for vested interests and in resolving the problem of NPLs can the framework for a new Japanese corporate governance system be created. Although it is not yet clear what the new governance system will entail, it will likely include a combination of main bank governance and governance

Table 6-4. *Expectations for Main Bank Financing, 1999*

	Companies capitalized	
Expectation	Less than ¥10 billion	More than ¥10 billion
Increase	13	12
No change	66	61
Decrease[a]	15	18
Undecided	6	9

Source: Japan, Ministry of Finance, *Wagaku ni Kigyo no Fainansu Shisutemu to Kōporeito Gabanasu ni Kansuru Ankei to Chōsan: Shukeikeka to Bunseki no Chukan Hōkoku* (General Finance Policy Research Center, November 1999).

a. Asked how they planned to make up for this decline, of companies capitalized under ¥10 billion, 75 percent said they would go to the market and 25 percent said they would go to other banks. For companies capitalized more than ¥10 billion, the figures were 88 percent and 13 percent, respectively.

through the market by institutional investors, such as insurance companies, trusts, and pensions. While this kind of change is occurring elsewhere in the world and some convergence of main bank and market-oriented economies seems inevitable, Japan will nonetheless chart its own course toward a new system of corporate governance.

7 Reopening Japan and Reforming the Foreign Policy Regime

Japan during the Edo period was described in chapter 3 as a nation of beauty and prosperity. Equally important, it was a nation of peace. The 265 years of peace that characterized the Edo civilization were deeply related to the isolationist system at the time. Internal and external peace were maintained in Japan, while much of the rest of the world was engaged in various conflicts, including the Seven Years' War in Europe, the U.S. War of Independence, the Napoleonic Wars that followed the French Revolution, the Spanish-American War, the Crimean War, and the French-Spanish War. This peace was possible in part because Japan is an island on the edge of the Asian continent, but more importantly because the government used its formidable political power to disarm the people and impose a policy of isolationism. Although the Japanese system was based on decentralization, the government had a monopoly on military and foreign policy, which was founded on isolationism and the policy of forced alternation of residences for the lords.[1] This

1. Shinzaburo Ōishi and Yūichi Ichimura, *Sakoku, Yuruyakana Jōhōkakumei* (Tokyo: Kōronsha Gendai Shinsho, 1995).

monopoly allowed the government to pursue a path of disarmament and peace.

At the time, Japan and Europe were comparably armed. Guns arrived in Japan in 1543 through the Portuguese, who landed on the island of Tanegashima; the War Period (from the mid-fifteenth to the early seventeenth century) was thus ripe for rapidly arming warriors with guns and cannons.[2] The victory of the Nobunaga Oda and Ieyasu Tokugawa alliance over Katsuyori Takeda in 1575, at Nagashino in Mikawa, was due to the use of guns.

Era of Peace and the Isolationist System

Japan eventually became a disarmed, peaceful nation, however, starting with Hideyoshi Toyotomi's land surveys and disarming of farmers, and the shrinking of the military in the Edo period. Although Japan produced a large amount of copper, the main element used in manufacturing weapons, most of it was exported. Because this revenue was not spent equipping the military, the Japanese rapidly accumulated wealth. In addition, the cultivation of rice paddies and nurturing of industries led to a sudden increase in agricultural productivity and an expansion in domestic demand, and Japan economically became a very wealthy nation. This was a peaceful and prosperous period that could be called *Pax Tokugawana.*

In terms of information and intelligence, isolationism was a "period when Japan was not 'transmitting' information but was assiduously 'receiving' information from abroad. At the center of it was the 'receipt' of information on the heretofore unknown region of Europe."[3] This reception-centered information system was not traditionally Japanese; it was one of the effects of the Edo period isolationism. As Ōishi stated:

> Historically, up to this point, Japan, which was in one corner of Asia, had from very early on involved itself internationally by sending students to China and by absorbing culture from the Korean Peninsula. In a sense, it had established its unique society in a sphere of Kanji culture. The sixteenth century exchange with Portugal and Spain of

---

2. The *Sengoku Jidai* (warring-states period) was a time of intense civil war in Japan, starting with the ten-year Onin War in 1467 and continuing until 1615, early in the Tokugawa period.

3. Ōishi and Ichimura, *Sakoku, Yuruyakana Jōhōkakumei*, p. 28 (my translation).

the European-Christian cultural sphere was pursued with incredible curiosity and cautiousness, to which the Oda-Toyotomi government and Ieyasu Tokugawa responded by "transmitting." However, under isolationism, the government created a system specifically for "reception" that made it possible to monopolize and manage the information and to accurately analyze the messages that were being received.[4]

In other words, although isolationist Japan created a mechanism for accurately receiving information from abroad, transmissions sent from Japan almost disappeared. Although the government largely revised the isolationist information reception-and-transmission system during the Meiji Restoration, the Edo period isolationism laid the foundation for the future Japanese foreign intelligence system. Particularly after the postwar period, as Japan reentered a period of peace under *Pax Americana*, this isolationist intelligence system became a common part of many Japanese institutions in a modified way.

Postwar Pacifism and Remilitarization

Seven years of allied occupation of Japan ended when the U.S.-Japan Peace Treaty was signed on September 8, 1951. On the same day, the signing of the U.S.-Japan Security Treaty established the framework for Japanese foreign relations in the postwar period. In the preceding months of negotiation, from January to August 1951, the issue of Japan's remilitarization was revisited several times. Then-U.S. secretary of state John Foster Dulles wanted to establish a modern army, navy, and air force and seriously rearm Japan. In word and deed, he wanted to work together with Japan to conclude a security treaty.

Hitoshi Ashida, a former prime minister (1948) also pushed for remilitarization. On December 7, 1950, he proposed the Ashida Opinion in which he pointed out that Article Nine of the Constitution did not prohibit rearming for the purpose of self-defense. He strongly advocated the creation of fifteen divisions of 200,000 men at military headquarters and he continued to pursue remilitarization in 1951. Following the direction of Ashida and the Democratic Party, eight business organizations, including

---

4. Ibid., pp. 197–98 (my translation). Kanji are pictographic characters that were imported from China to form the basis of the Japanese writing system.

the Keidanren, also called for the "formation of a small but efficient military organization," and Ichiro Hatoyama stressed the necessity of remilitarization to Dulles.[5]

However, then-Prime Minister Shigeru Yoshida opposed remilitarization using public opinion as a shield and solving the domestic security problem by creating a police contingency force. Despite being a conservative, he chose to cooperate with the pacifist progressive majority in Japan. He thought that if U.S. forces were stationed in Japan it would directly or indirectly prevent invasion from the east. A compromise was reached; Japan would not remilitarize but would instead rely on the United States to provide for its defense through the security treaty.[6]

This compromise prompted criticism from both conservatives and progressives. Ashida and his Democratic Party, as well as the Hatoyama Group of the Liberal Party, publicly called for remilitarization under a new constitution. At the same time, communist and socialist parties and the progressive intelligentsia criticized Yoshida's path as that of a dependent, or only half-independent, nation. However, Shigeru Yoshida's intention was not to remain unarmed indefinitely but rather to respond pragmatically to the situation and gradually remilitarize. Considering the political situation at the beginning of the 1950s and the strong influence of the pacifist progressives on the general public, Yoshida's decision was not a foolish one for a politician at that time. However, in appearing to accept the progressives' logic on the surface, he actually established realism and pragmatism as the principles of postwar conservative politics. Although Yoshida made political compromises, he probably had not sacrificed his conservative ideals. Ironically his compromises changed the characteristics of Japanese conservatism: although the Liberal Democratic Party, which was created in 1955 from an alliance of conservative parties, made the enactment of a new Japanese constitution and subsequent remilitarization the goal of the party, the goal eroded over time.

As Yoshida expected, remilitarization did move forward. Although there were various legal restrictions and heavy dependence on the U.S. military, the Japanese forces became a near-professional military. With the disintegration of socialism, the progressives eventually became more realistic and,

---

5. Hatoyama was a former prime minister who served three times between 1954 and 1956.

6. The security treaty stipulated that U.S. forces were to be stationed in Japan but were not specifically obligated to defend Japan. Providing defense, however, was an option. Furthermore, the area of responsibility did not limit itself to Japan but extended to the Far East.

under the Murayama government, even the socialists came to accept the idea of self-defense forces.

In hindsight, the issue was not remilitarization, but rather the fundamental question of Japanese independence and a new opening of the country. This included rethinking both the nature of the Constitution after the occupation and the wisdom of completely depending upon another country for defense. While postponing resolution of this fundamental issue created a problem at the core of the postwar Japanese political and economic systems, it also made high growth possible. In this way, the postwar period characterized by pacifism and high growth was similar to the Edo period, when the focus on rice cultivation and the nurturing of industry under a long-term peace and demilitarization policy led to a long period of prosperity.

U.S.-Dependent Isolationism

Having depended unilaterally on the United States for defense under the U.S.-Japan Security Treaty and having been put in the position of military and political semi-independence, Japan entered into the cold war structure in a state of U.S.-dependent isolationism. In the bipolar system, Japan was able to manage internationally and economically as long as it maintained a strong relationship with the United States.

The nature of this isolation was not characterized by the limitation of the import and export of goods or money, but was rather "information isolation."[7] The isolation came from the fact that the flow of information was limited, unless it came through the United States. The reception system for information through the United States was well developed, whereas there was almost no mechanism for its transmission. This was very similar to the government system during the Edo period. However, one difference from the Edo period system was that it was the Foreign Ministry that tried, for the most part successfully, to monopolize information from abroad, mainly from the United States. While economic information was accessible for civilians and other ministries, military, political and strategic information was concentrated for the most part in the Foreign Ministry.

---

7. The use of the word *information* in this context includes the concept of intelligence, from which Japan was also isolated.

Japanese pacifism, or rather the political system based on the postwar Constitution that embodied pacifism, largely limited the collection of information it deemed necessary for national security, whether it was for the military or civilians. Because Japan was "determined to preserve [its] security and existence, trusting in the justice and faith of the peace-loving peoples of the world," it was considered unnecessary to collect information on the treacherous activities of other countries.[8] Information and intelligence services were thought to be unnecessary in postwar Japan; instead, the Foreign Ministry selectively distributed this type of information obtained from the United States. In most countries, regional research is deeply connected to intelligence gathering for national security; however, in postwar Japan, there were almost no intelligence activities and regional research declined rapidly.

The weakened military and nonmilitary intelligence activities indirectly diminished the strategic aspect of information. The media portrayed the government and other institutions' strategic information gathering as an evil that was contrary to pacifism. As a result, the information system leaned heavily toward economic activities. The postwar information isolation, which began with the weakening of the military, foreign, and intelligence capability, eventually permeated all aspects of Japanese society.

An additional reason for the isolation was Japan's weakness in foreign languages. The Japanese media, which was protected by the nontariff barrier of the Japanese language, had little foreign competition and created an oligopolistic market that was extremely domestically oriented. Although some U.S. news was reported, there was very limited information about other areas of the world. Furthermore, throughout the postwar period, there were very few transmissions of reports from Japan to the rest of the world. In other countries, the U.S.-produced *International Herald Tribune* and the U.K.-produced *Financial Times* were widely read; in Japan, the readership was very small. Japan also failed to take advantage of the availability of what were considered common sources of information in other countries, such as CNN, BBC, and CNBC, which have solidified their positions in the international television media in the last ten years.

The Japanese are often criticized for their lack of internationalism and their close-minded or island mentality. The reason is not that Japanese culture, economics, or social systems are inherently isolationist, but that

---

8. Quote is from the preface to the Constitution of Japan, promulgated November 3, 1946. The English version is available at www.shugiin.go.jp/itdb_main.nsf/html/index_e_kenpou.htm.

because of its information isolation, Japan is unable to share in international information exchange, and therefore its decisionmaking processes and modes of behavior are naturally domestically oriented. Before World War II, Japan interacted with the colonies of Korea, Taiwan, and Manchuria, and even with South America because of emigration. After its defeat, however, Japan's information isolation was strengthened by the loss of colonies and the resulting decrease in contact. Although the West also had lost colonies, in the case of the victors, international communication was maintained and given an appropriate role in postwar international political and economic strategy.

For Japan, where everything from the prewar period was rejected, and for Japanese democracy, which had undergone criticism to the point of self-torment over the invasion of Asia, it was out of the question to maintain contact to gather information. The only successful postwar Japanese intellectual exchange was with the United States. The educational exchange system was continuously maintained through programs such as the Fulbright Fellowship. Much information flowed into Japan from the United States through those programs. Although the information exchange was concentrated in the social sciences, such as economics, management, political science, and sociology, the United States had an incredible influence on almost all academic fields. U.S. cultural attitudes also became an important source of information and knowledge as disseminated by exchange students returning from the United States. While the United States had enormous influence in politics and academia, European and Asian influence was negligible.

Isolationist Immigration Policy

In the postwar period, the information isolationist policy was supplemented by a human isolationist policy. Despite the free flow of goods and services that occurred after World War II, countries were more cautious regarding the liberalization of labor. This was a very different development from the emphasis on the (sometimes forced) immigration that occurred during nineteenth-century globalization. With the intensification of globalization and the information technology revolution in the 1980s and 1990s Europe moved toward deregulation with the establishment of the European Union, and the United States did likewise with the passage of the North American Free Trade Agreement (NAFTA). Japan was the only country that maintained severe immigration laws, such as the Nationality Act and the Immigration Act.

This human isolation policy is strongly related to the medium- and long-term trends of the Japanese economy. Japan is an aging society with a low birthrate, and there is no indication that the decreasing birthrate will reverse. At a time when Japanese women are rapidly making advances in society and gender equality is becoming increasingly important, it is unlikely there will be an increase in the birthrate. Society is certain to continue aging, which will lead to the weakening of the economy. The most viable policy option is the dissolution of the human isolation policy and an increase in the proportion of émigrés to Japan (in terms of both the labor force and the citizenry) on par with the United States and Europe.

Although many Japanese do not know it, Japan's legal structure is extremely exclusionary toward foreigners. In determining nationality, Japan uses parentage as the criterion, unlike the United States, United Kingdom, and Australia, which use birthplace, so it is difficult to obtain Japanese citizenship. Furthermore, even if all of the objective requirements for naturalization are met, it is still necessary to have the consent of the Minister of Justice. In addition, the third requirement for naturalization is good behavior, which is very subjective and leaves a lot of room for administrative discretion. This is in contrast to the U.S. system where the requirements for naturalization are specific and clear, where those who fulfill necessary requirements are allowed to become citizens by law, and where the final legal decision is left to the courts.

Japanese immigration law, in principle, does not allow the entry of manual laborers. Although entry is possible for those who wish to conduct research or other nonmanual labor, manual laborers must receive special limited permission, which is only exceptionally granted. Even though it is possible for foreigners with specific skills, abilities, and knowledge to enter the country as nonmanual laborers if their particular skills are included on the official list, it is impossible for a person with an unlisted profession, such as a hospice nurse, to enter without a change in the law. These stringent legal restrictions are normally justified for national security or social security reasons, but clearly that is not always the case.

It is said that behind the United States' strong growth and increase in productivity during the 1990s was a culture that embraced competition. One of the necessary elements of such a culture is an open entry policy that includes immigration. Much of the technological innovation in the United States is driven by foreigners, including Asian-Americans (mainly Indian-Americans and Chinese-Americans). For example, without the systems engineers, many of whom are Indian-American, Silicon Valley would not have enjoyed the prosperity that it has. If Japan were to change its immigration policies to allow Chinese venture capitalists and Indian systems engineers to stay for a longer term, it would provide an economic boost similar to the one the United States experienced. In this period of information revolution and globalization, specialized knowledge and the ability to organize it is strategically necessary. Fundamentally reforming laws such as the Nationality Act and the Immigration Act and ending human isolationism is thus increasingly becoming an important objective. Japan's strict and administratively nontransparent rules strengthen bureaucratic authority and increase the power of the *yakuza* and other organized crime syndicates. While there are advantages to isolation, such as a comfortable and harmonious social system, its disadvantages are too great. If Japan does not discard the comfort of isolation, it will fall behind the rest of the world economically, and socially it will rapidly lose vitality.

Reevaluating the "Number Two Strategy"

Japan's postwar foreign policy strategy of supporting the United States while striving to economically catch up to, and eventually surpass, the West made it the number two economic power and thus had merit for both Japan and the United States, as well as for neighboring Asian countries. Japan emphasized its importance as a strategic economic ally to the United States and used economic aid to complement the United States' position as a superpower. Therefore, while maintaining a policy of isolationism with regard to people and information and viewing the world through the window of the United States, Japan through the use of economic aid was able to function as a member of the global community.

While the "number two strategy" was a success during the cold war, the changes since have fundamentally affected Japan's foreign policy environment. The shift from a bipolar to a multipolar structure, as well as the increase in globalization and the advent of the information revolution, altered the hierarchical hegemony, and Japan no longer needed to choose between allying with the United States versus the USSR versus Asia. Under network globalization, even a superpower is only one of the focal points of the network, albeit an important one.

Japan must thus rethink its strategy. In a multipolar world, Japan must share values with many countries in many ways, and not just with the

United States, as fixed and exclusive alliances can be a drawback. This would be a sort of "reopening" of Japan, which would entail pursuing bilateral and regional efforts without the United States. This does not imply that the U.S.-Japan Security Treaty must be abandoned. However, it is clear that the foreign policy that maintained isolationism while adopting the U.S. view of the world must be reevaluated.

Because this proposal may be interpreted as a challenge to U.S. hegemony, several key players involved with foreign relations, including the Ministry of Foreign Affairs, have been opposed to such a change. This opposition is largely based on bureaucratic inertia. Japan could become an information-based network society, and the notion of alignment with a hegemon would become outdated. Samuel Huntington calls the twenty-first century the era of "clashing civilizations," and Nobuo Noda calls it the period of "new empires."[9] In other words, the world is moving away from an era dominated by ideology and nation states to a period in which gentle but far-reaching orders of culture and empires dominate. This is also a move away from Western domination and toward non-Western, postmodern societies. As Andre Gunder Frank noted, it is time for a change in direction from the West to the East.[10] As the only Asian country to succeed at modernization, Japan has a large handicap in the twenty-first century. Noda adds:

> In order for the Japanese not to continue wandering aimlessly in the twenty-first century, it is necessary to analytically recognize the "historical evolution" of East Asia. In addition, it is necessary to strive to establish a wide-reaching order in Asia with Japan in a strong position, while incorporating the regional imperial influences of the United States, Russia, and Central Europe. To this end, it is normal that there should be wide-reaching concepts of economics and security. At the same time, efforts are necessary to discover universal elements in Japanese culture that can be widely applied. This is because the currently progressing reorganization of imperialist world order has cultural conflicts at its base.[11]

9. Samuel P. Huntington, "The Clash of Civilizations?" *Foreign Affairs* (Summer 1993), pp. 22–49; Nobuo Noda, *Nijyusēki o dō Miruka* (Tokyo: Bunshushinsho, 1998).

10. Andre Gunder Frank, *Reorient: Global Economy in the Asian Age* (University of California Press, 1998).

11. Noda, *Nijyusēki o dō Miruka*, pp. 218–19 (my translation).

If Japan were able to truly become open and develop the universal elements of its culture in a multipolar world, as pointed out by Noda, it could have a significant role in the future of Asia. This cannot happen if the previous Japan-centered "building of a new Asian order" continues. Because Japan is an outlying country, it can play a particular role in the complex interactions between China, India, and Southeast Asian countries. As an important focal point in the Asian subsystem, or Asian network, Japan's significance can and should be maintained.

Although Japan exists in the East Asian cultural belt with China and the Korean Peninsula, it nonetheless needs to work on cultural and economic networks with Southeast Asia and South Asia with India at the center. To create a balanced new order in Asia, it is important to have a network linking Korea, Japan, Southeast Asia, and India, with China at the center. To accomplish this, Japan must reorganize Asia's various and complex cultures and history and conduct foreign policy that is versatile and vital.

Some think that this will be difficult for Japan because of the continued isolation of its people and its isolation from information. However, the Japanese have historically demonstrated an advanced ability to absorb and apply foreign cultures and, even now, it has this cultural flexibility. The problem is that Japan has lost the will and the necessary language ability to continue to do this because of its pursuit of the Number Two Strategy. "For half a century, [Japan] has judged its relationship with Asian countries along the time trajectory of development," Yonosuke Hara says. "To put it succinctly, under the world order offered by the United States, Japan did not project any words of its own but concentrated on directing money that Asia needed through both public and private channels."[12]

The time when overseas development assistance and private direct investment were adequate to maintain a relationship with the rest of Asia is over. Japan needs to take many steps if it is to develop a new Asian foreign policy for the twenty-first century. These should include the development of more imaginative relationships, the continuation of network building, and the nurturing of talent. The first reforms associated with these steps should include a fundamental review of the current foreign policy system in the Ministry of Foreign Affairs, the formulation of a new paradigm, and the rebuilding of personnel infrastructure to support the new paradigm.

---

12. Yonosuke Hara, *Asiagata Kēzai System—Globalism ni Kōshite* (Tokyo: Chūkōshinsha, 2000), p. 175 (my translation).

Reevaluating Centralized Diplomacy
and the Creation of an Intelligence Agency

The main problem in the postwar foreign policy system was that there was a lack of strategic thinking in foreign policy itself, and consequently strategic information was not seriously sought. This was the result of Shigeru Yoshida's decision to pursue a pragmatic U.S.-dependent national security and foreign relations policy after the war. Under this policy, the Foreign Ministry did not have a lot of room to maneuver. High-level active and former Foreign Ministry officials have publicly stated that there was no other strategy for Japan besides alliance with the United States and Anglo-Saxon countries; these statements implied that this strategy had frozen the thinking in the institution. The result was that the Foreign Ministry, or a large part of it, gave up collecting strategic international information and depended solely on intelligence provided at the discretion of the United States. Instead, the Foreign Ministry pursued an "entertainment foreign policy" that focused on parties and dinners. Foreign Ministry scandals, such as the slush fund and the personal use of budget resources, are also characteristic symptoms of the organizational rot resulting from an entertainment foreign policy.

Although pacifism is still strong and there is opposition to the reorganization and expansion of the Defense Agency and the Prime Minister's Office, a strategic information agency that also deals with military intelligence needs to be created outside of the Foreign Ministry. At a time when a new far-reaching order is being formed, it is normal and necessary for Japan to have an intelligence agency, particularly if Japan is to be independent. The Foreign Ministry must cooperate with this new intelligence agency and work to gather strategic information.

The Foreign Ministry's other major problem is that it has tried to monopolize foreign relations under centralized diplomacy at a time when globalization has been rapidly spreading through networks. The Foreign Ministry cannot centralize foreign relations when trade, capital, and human networks are becoming global. The Ministry of Economy, Trade, and Industry should be responsible for trade; the Ministry of Finance should be in charge of currency diplomacy; and the Ministry of the Environment should take the lead in environmental diplomacy. Although it is logical that the Cabinet manages and centrally directs the affairs of state, there is no need for the Ministry of Foreign Affairs to centralize control of all foreign relations. Even though it is the government and Foreign Ministry's job to support private sector activity, the private sector has its own networks for conducting international business. Trying to centralize and manage this reflects archaic thinking.

Under the slogan of diplomatic centralization, the ministry fundamentally monopolizes ambassadorial and ministerial personnel issues, with some minor exceptions. Because ambassadors are special government officials, for practical reasons the Prime Minister's Office should handle appointments. The influence of the prime minister and his office should also be strengthened with regard to personnel below the ministerial level. At least half of the ambassadors should be appointed from other ministries or from the private sector. Because the private sector conducts much of Japan's foreign activity, and most intergovernmental relations exist outside of the Foreign Ministry, it is appropriate that the makeup of personnel reflect that fact.

Japan's neglect in collecting strategic information has also had consequences in terms of the weakness of academic area studies. Ordinarily, area studies develop along with intelligence activities, yet in postwar Japan, the government gave very little incentive or support for regional studies. Even in the Foreign Ministry, those who specialized in countries other than the United States, Europe, China, and Russia were not nurtured. Although specialists have been employed as professional researchers, they have been harshly discriminated against in terms of career advancement. Given the importance of other Asian countries to Japan, it is very troubling that there are so few diplomats who speak the local languages in countries such as Indonesia, Thailand, Malaysia, and Myanmar. The negative consequences of giving abnormal levels of privilege to diplomats and discriminating against specialists are significant. Having eliminated the diplomatic examination system, the Foreign Ministry should strengthen its nurturing of specialists by allowing them to become ambassadors. For example, appointing a sitting ambassador to Thailand who can speak Thai and is knowledgeable about Thai history would have immeasurable direct and indirect benefits. It is thus important to create incentives for area studies by changing personnel policies.

Japan's dependency on the United States has created a foreign policy infrastructure that is centered on the United States and Europe. The postwar distribution of embassies and consulates has not changed significantly despite the world's changing. For example, Japan has eighteen consulates and an embassy in the United States, but often has one embassy that serves multiple countries in the Balkans, Central Asia, and Africa.[13] In smaller countries, the ambassador has a larger role, while in the United States and Europe the role that embassies and ambassadors play is greatly diminishing. In larger countries, corporations have their own subsidiaries and local businesses, and thus require less support from embassies. Despite this unequal distribution and the advisability of redistributing its embassies from the West to Asia and other developing countries, there is almost no discussion of such policy reform.

It is time for Japan to shift its U.S.-dependent foreign policy to one more balanced between East and West and to move away from the centralized diplomacy of the Ministry of Foreign Affairs. Only in this way will Japan be able to emerge from isolation and take its place as an independent and fully functioning member of the Asian region and the global community.

---

13. The eighteen consulates in the United States include those in Guam and Saipan.

8 | The Formation of the Japanese Meritocracy System

By establishing a thorough meritocracy and an education system based on equal opportunity, the Meiji
leaders sought to actualize the revolution of social hierarchy.
The meritocracy created and established in Japan was one
based on academic background.[1] During the hundred years
after the Meiji period, this academic-background meritocracy became the foundation of the Japanese social system,
thereby planting the ideology of self-advancement—even
among ordinary citizens.

It was Takato Ōki who set up the real education system
during the Meiji period. In August 1872, he wrote the following in the official document promulgating the fundamental ideas behind the education system: "[People] should
study according to their ability, dedicate themselves to it,

---

1. Japan's meritocracy was based on a concept called *gakureki*. *Gakureki
Shakai* is a society based on people's academic background (literally, "school history") where the utmost value is placed on the school (specifically, the university)
from which a person graduates. In Japan, these elite universities include Tokyo,
Kyoto, Keio, and Waseda. Since the Meiji Era, most government ministries and
the largest corporations have selected their management-track employees almost
exclusively from these universities. This practice was started in an effort to eliminate nepotism in Japanese society.

leave a legacy, build a fortune, and work hard; education is the foundation of success and wealth," and "'all humans' should obtain an education."[2]

Hirofumi Itō and Arinori Mori were the ones who finished developing the education system that Ōki had started. Although Mori was from the Satsuma domain, in 1884 when he was the Minister to England, he met Itō and they spoke about the education problem. Itō, who was impressed by Mori's knowledge, appointed him as the first Minister of Education. Mori created the higher education system with the Imperial University at the top. Through this system and with the abolition of the social hierarchy and affiliation systems, there was an attempt to create and nurture systemic elites of post-Meiji Japan through equal opportunity. With the support of this education system and the dissolution of the social hierarchy system that the Meiji leaders were striving for, it was possible to establish a society without classes and with high social mobility.

Dissolution of the Academic-Background Meritocracy

This academic-background meritocracy, however, is now falling apart. Not only have no new criteria been created to take the place of Japanese meritocracy, but there is also a deepening confusion caused by the lack of a new sense of direction. Hideki Wada writes about the reality of the collapse of the academic-background meritocracy and its state of crisis. He believes that twenty-first century Japan will see the end of a society based on academic background. When Wada was a child, parents of wealthy households were doctors and elite salaried workers and children recognized the value of studying hard in order to enter a top-notch school that would eventually lead to a good job. However, during the bubble era, students began to recognize that this path could no longer guarantee them a high standard of living. In Wada's mind, this change of viewpoint was only natural because the children of parents who graduated from an elite school, such as Tokyo University, were living in cramped apartments far from Tokyo while children whose parents were merchants were much better off.

"[S]ince then, with nepotism being taken for granted by company presidents, politicians, and even celebrities, the value of an educational pedigree has definitely fallen in the last ten years," Wada goes on to say. "Education is no longer an effective tool for shaping one's own future. Parents

---

2. Ikuo Amano, *Shiken no Shakaishi—Kindainihon no Shiken, Kyōiku, Shakai* (Tokyo: Tokyo University Press, 1983), p. 66 (my translation).

and children feel that Japan has become a nepotistic society like that of the West."[3]

While the dissolution of the Japanese capitalist system in the context of globalization and the information and telecommunication revolution may also have been reasons for the collapse of the academic-background meritocracy, the "education reform" proposed by the Ministry of Education and Science is the primary reason.[4] This education reform stood in opposition to educational pedigree in general, and Tokyo University in particular, as well as the examination process. In doing so, it has contributed a great deal to the destruction of Japanese meritocracy. With an overload of information from the media describing the harmful effects of the examination process and with the support of the postwar Japanese ideology of equality of results, the assault on academic-background meritocracy became fashionable. The Ministry of Education and Science and some intellectuals joined the movement and pushed for "reform," the result of which is that the Japanese education meritocracy is now being destroyed.

Results of Egalitarianism and Denial of Competition

The point of reform, the Provisional Council on Educational Reform said in its 1985 report, was to "correct the harm of the academic-background society" and "fix the intensifying examination hell."[5] Elaborating its view of an academic-background society, it said:

> The harm of the academic-background society is not limited to today's education and learning system; because it is rooted in social customs and human behavior, there are many aspects that will be resolved in the long-term in the context of building a society of life-long learning. Along with this, a comprehensive policy of reform is necessary from three aspects: schools, businesses, and the bureaucracy.[6]

Our "socialistic" education administration rejects objective conceptualization of "ability" and the notion of deciding through a dialogue with

---

3. Hideki Wada, *Gakuryokuhōkai* (Tokyo: PHP Kenkyūjo, 1999), pp. 10–11 (my translation).

4. The full name is the Ministry of Education, Culture, Sports, Science and Technology (as of January 2001). In this book, the name is shortened to Ministry of Education and Science in the interest of brevity.

5. Provisional Council on Educational Reform, "Report on Educational Reform, Part One" (June 26, 1985), pp. 4–5 (my translation).

6. Ibid.

society just what that would be. Furthermore, the education bureaucrats are moving in the direction of rejecting the concept of "ability" itself, as well as that of competition.

The rejection of the notions of ability and competition has resulted in the disappearance of differences in quality and the rejection of competition in public high schools, which are areas where the Board of Education and the Ministry of Education and Science have the most authority. With such an education system, it is only natural for the social system to lean toward nepotism and hereditary succession rather than ability. What do the socialistic education bureaucrats think of young people who are skilled at "brown-nosing" and not inclined to do substantive work?

In chapter 4 it was noted that 90 percent of employment is under a socialistic system, and there is a dual structure in Japanese politics and economics. Education, however, is even more socialistic than that. Despite the fact that agriculture, public works, and the small retail sector exist in the context of stringent regulation and subsidy, these sectors have been influenced by the market and by competition. In comparison, even though education has been shaken by the market influences on cram schools, the socialistic system has been fundamentally maintained through strong management and control.[7] This has been possible because, relative to other areas, the deregulation of education has not moved forward.

Reevaluating Socialistic Education Policy

The goal of school education (mainly primary and secondary education) is to teach at least the minimum amount of knowledge young people need to live in Japanese society and, furthermore, to make routine the use of that knowledge as a base from which they can learn on their own and think on their own (mainly during high school education).

To achieve this end, it is essential that Japan implement genuine reform rather than the Ministry of Education and Science's present "education reform," which has been a change for the worse. As a way to round out educational "reform" based on egalitarianism and the rejection of compe-

7. Cram schools (*juku* in Japanese) are after-school programs attended by students seeking extra tutelage in math, science, Japanese language, and other subjects in which they are having difficulty in their regular school. Students also attend to prepare for the very difficult entrance exams to enter junior high school, high school, and university. In 2000, cram school enrollment was approximately 29 percent for elementary school, 57 percent for lower secondary school, and 31 percent for upper secondary school students. Japan Information Network (JIN), http://jin.jcic.or.jp/stat/stats/16EDUA1.html.

tition, the Ministry of Education and Science is implementing what it calls a "new" curriculum. This "reform" that is being carried out in order to pursue education with *yutori* includes elements that could completely destroy the basic functioning of elementary and junior high education.[8] If we are truly concerned for the essential nature of Japanese education and want to implement genuine reform rather than something that is a change for the worse, we must first prevent the use of the new curriculum.

Genuine reform would have the goal of creating a meritocracy appropriate to today's new environment that would replace the old meritocracy. However, this must begin with a change in education administration and its socialistic education system. And in order to accomplish this, the appropriate legal structure must be changed because Japan's administration is managed through laws, ordinances, and administrative guidance. The various ministries have basic laws related to their appropriate administrative areas. Furthermore, specific regulations and ordinances, as well as guidance, are prescribed and issued based on such laws.

Having defined the objective of education reform as the teaching of knowledge and the advancement of scholastic aptitude, the next point is to discuss how Japanese education policy should be changed so that those goals can be met, or, more specifically, how the School Education Law and related laws and regulations should be changed.

Establishing Choice in Education

While it is not possible to discuss the actual revision of laws here, the point is to expand the choice for students and allow schools, particularly universities and graduate schools, to be truly independent and to manage themselves. With regard to the establishment of schools, the process should be based on registration and standards should be transparent and in the form of listed criteria. If the Ministry of Education and Science evaluates whether academic standards are being met and publicizes those results, and students and their families are allowed to choose freely among schools, natural selection will pinpoint the problem schools. If the distribution of funding to schools is tied to results, schools that cannot attain satisfactory results will not be able to continue financially.

---

8. *Yutori* literally means to have time or space. With regard to education, it refers to a style of education that gives children time and emotional space and is not challenging or competitive. The Ministry of Education and Science translates *yutori* as "room to grow."

Along those lines, it would be appropriate for each board of education, or even each school, to determine what subjects should be taught at the elementary, middle, and high school levels and, thus, eliminate the practice of having the Minister of Education and Science make that determination. However, the Ministry should set the minimum standard for teaching and the results should be evaluated by nationwide testing. Recently, the former deputy minister of education Motoyuki Ono has said he wants the new curriculum, which was implemented starting in April 2002, to be the minimum standard. Of course, it is a theoretical contradiction to maintain central authority over the curriculum on one hand and to have minimum standards on the other, but this would only be a temporary means of addressing the immediate situation.

With regard to the management of schools, it is important for the management authority of principals to be strengthened and for their responsibilities to be clear. Currently, a wide range of authority, such as that over personnel, is given to local boards of education. Much of that authority should be given to the schools and their management. Although the personnel authority over principals and their deputies should be left to local boards of education, personnel authority over teachers should be given to the schools. It is impossible to have management without authority over personnel. Accordingly, article 59 of the School Education Law should be repealed and important management authority, such as that over faculty, should be given to presidents of universities and university management. The authority of university presidents and university management should be reviewed and monitored by a separate committee. Moreover, the Ministry of Education and Science should establish transparent evaluation standards, evaluate universities, and publicize those results.

It is clear that in order to dramatically reform education policy with regard to school education, the School Education Law, and its related regulations and ordinances, including the Ministry of Education and Science Establishment Law, must be revised for the better.[9] Though I am not opposed to revising the Basic Education Law, it should be done as a part of larger constitutional reform rather than as a part of education reform. With

9. What is unique about the Ministry of Education and Science, compared with other ministries, is that it has a Basic Education Law. As is widely known, the Basic Education Law was approved along with the Japanese Constitution in March 1947. It is understood to be the basic law containing the fundamental principles of the education system and is binding on the implementation and interpretation of other education laws. In a sense, it was a preamble to the education law that lays out the core philosophy of education.

regard to education reform, it would be more effective to focus on laws other than the Basic Education Law, for example, the School Education Law. For those who do not want laws and ordinances or education administration to be changed, the desire is to place the focus on the Basic Education Law so that the pressure for genuine reform is eased; it is for this very reason that the focus should not be placed on the revision of the Basic Education Law.

Centralization vs. Decentralization

As can be observed from the School Education Law and the Private School Education Law, Japanese education and its implementing organs (that is, schools) are under very strict regulation and direction by the Ministry of Education and Science. Indeed, some regulations are necessary in education because education is a public good and some schooling is compulsory. The issue here is not the ideological dichotomy of regulation and liberalization or market and government, but rather what amount of regulation and direction is appropriate? This question can be divided into two parts. The first is how much regulation and direction should be centralized and how much should be decentralized. With regard to the current system, the issue is which aspects of regulation and direction should be conducted at the central government level and which should be left to local boards of education. The issue of further decentralization of authority from local boards of education to the individual principals is another very important aspect of decentralization.

The second part of the question is how much should be left to market principles and market competition. Now, at a time when variety and innovation are valued in education, the market has more than a small role to play, as seen from education reforms in the United Kingdom and the United States.[10] It is very important to allow competition and the market

10. As is evident from the United Kingdom, for example, the decentralization of power from the central government to the localities and from the localities to the schools and the use of market principles are closely connected. This is because without the foundation of self-management through creativity and effort, there is no way to implement market mechanisms. While pursuing strong decentralization, the central education bureau has shown strong leadership by establishing national standards and by evaluating and publicizing results. On this point, U.S. education reform, which was started in the 1980s, is similar. The last twenty years of reform seem to have included two basic elements: one is the top-down establishment of standards for educational substance and scholastic ability, and the development and administering of scholastic aptitude tests based on those standards; the other is the bottom-up deciphering of appropriate reforms at the school level based on deregulation.

to play an appropriate role within education as a practical matter, considering that various reforms already have been carried out by cram schools, which are outside the regulation of the Ministry of Education and Science.

One of the reforms that has been receiving attention is the establishment of charter schools. Mutsuhisa Kishimoto stated the following with regard to the connection between education reform and charter schools: "In the context of moving forward in implementing reform with uniformity, standardization, and deregulation at its core, the primary historical factor for the appearance of charter schools is the strengthening policy direction of clarifying each school's responsibility for educational results."[11] Establishing national education standards and clarifying the schools' responsibility for results, then pursuing complete decentralization and deregulation is curiously similar to the education reforms carried out in the United Kingdom.

On the other hand, in the administration of Japanese education, it is the center that determines the uniform national scholastic teaching methodology through the establishment of national standards. While, in this sense, it might be said that Japan is ahead of the United Kingdom and the United States, it is problematic that the national standard has continued to fall for the last twenty years and that there have been no national tests to evaluate whether the standards have been met. A further problem is that the way to meet the standards (for example, details of subjects and approval of textbooks) is highly restricted and only limited autonomy is given to schools and communities in this regard.

There is debate about whether to apply the U.S. and U.K. reform and charter school experiments in Japan. Is the collapse, or near collapse, of the Japanese education system not proof, however, that in spite of uniform national standards, there is no evaluation of their attainment, and that there is no option but to continuously and dramatically decrease the level of the standard? If the existing system already had positive results, there would be no reason to discuss market mechanisms just for the purpose of ideological debate. However, since centralized power and national regulation are causing the system to malfunction, the situation is more serious. Like the socialist system in the former Union of Soviet Socialist Republics (USSR) that collapsed in the 1990s, necessitating the creation of a new sys-

---

11. Mutsuhisa Kishimoto, "Charter School no Sēdoteki Tokuchō to Jittai," in Gendai America Kyōiku Kenkyūkai, *Gakushūsha no Needs ni Taiō suru America no Chōsen* (Tokyo: Kyōikukaihatsukenkyūjo, 2000), p. 54 (my translation).

tem altogether, the socialistic education policies of the Ministry of Education and Science must also be completely revised.

Increasing the Level of Knowledge and Scholastic Aptitude

In this situation, what should be the goal in reforming the socialistic education policy? First, reform with regard to education policy should be limited to school education reform. Based on two reports of the fifteenth session of the Central Council for Education, the Ministry of Education and Science has stated that the goal of school education from now on would be to teach "zest for living."[12] This objective, however, completely misses the mark. First of all, the concept of zest for living is abstract and open to subjective judgment, making it difficult to evaluate and impossible to determine whether, and to what extent, the goal has been reached. Choosing a concept that cannot be evaluated as the goal of school education may be a subconscious expression of the fact that those who are responsible really do not want to change anything specific. The other major problem with this goal is that the concept of zest for living is in large part the antithesis of scholastic training and study.

While the limitations of time and space prevent addressing here each point that needs to be changed, it should be clear that the principles laid out here for education reform and education policy reform would be a radical systemic transformation. In essence, students and parents would have more freedom to choose schools and schools would have real management authority. Of course, it goes without saying that the Ministry of Education and Science would set the minimum national standards and evaluate schools based on those standards, which assumes the implementation of market mechanisms through liberalization. While this is similar to the immense task of transforming a socialistic economic system into a market system, this is not based on the belief that markets are the answer to everything.

12. Japan, Ministry of Education, Culture, Sports, Science and Technology, "The Model for Japanese Education in the Perspective of the 21st Century: First Report by the Central Council for Education," July 19, 1996, and "Second Report by the Central Council for Education," June 26, 1997. "Zest for living" (*Ikiru Chikara*) is defined as "the ability to identify problems for oneself, learn for oneself, think for oneself, make independent judgments and actions and solve problems well; these are its important pillars, and in order to cultivate 'zest for living,' we would like to point out the indispensable aim of further advancing a way of thinking that respects individuality" ("Second Report," chap. 1).

Although it is clear that meritocracy based on academic background can no longer keep up with the substantial changes currently taking place in the context of globalization, the current trend to replace it with egalitarianism is misguided. The present times call for replacing the academic-background meritocracy with a different type of meritocracy. Here the Ministry of Education and Science can still have a fundamental role: that of shaping the substance of what the new meritocracy will become.

The challenge is to find the appropriate balance among the roles of the government, the people, and the market.

9 | The Central versus Local Government Debate

Nearly half a century has passed since the Japanese Constitution mandated the decentralization of authority to local governments, and twenty years have passed since the government decided that the "age of the local community" would be one of the government's policy objectives. At least on the surface, the decentralization of authority has continued as one of Japan's postwar ideologies and, as such, has very seldom been criticized.

There is now a need to revitalize the provinces and rebuild local communities, and opportunities for this are finally beginning to appear. Before acting upon these opportunities, there is a need to revisit the ideology of decentralization and thoroughly analyze the current situation in order to figure out how specifically to reform the regional system.

The Myth of the Central Government State

First, there must be a clear understanding of the state of central and regional authority and how finance is structured. Then, the issue of centralization and decentralization

111

of power must be analyzed apart from ideology. Michio Muramatsu calls the basic model for decentralization of power the "vertical administrative control model," which he says has three characteristics:[1]

—Administration is the important element of the relationship between the center and the local levels, and politics is only secondary.

—Local level decisions go through administrative channels to the central ministry and are regulated through the ministry's local control office.

—The government is the nexus that connects the will of the central ministries with that of the local governments and transmits a strengthened sense of sectionalism from the center to the local level.

Thus, according to this model, the central bureaucracy's control over local governments has not changed since the Meiji period. The postwar dissolution of the Ministry of the Interior resulted in bringing the sectionalism of the central bureaucracy into local governments.

Akira Amakawa has categorized the various types of central and local government relationships relative to two axes: centralization versus decentralization and separation versus interfusion:

> Centralization is where the decisions regarding the local government are made by the central government and where the central government narrows the area where local communities and citizens can decide for themselves; on the other hand, decentralization is where the autonomy of local communities and citizens is expanded. [Separation is where] the central government institution manages the central government's function independently of that of the local community even though the issue is within the local community's domain; [interfusion is where] even if it is a function of the central government, if it is in the local community's domain, the local community works with the appropriate administrative central government institution.[2]

Under these categories, the central-local relationship under the Meiji Constitution was one of centralization and interfusion, while the vertical administrative control model of the postwar period is one of centralization

1. Michio Muramatsu, "Chuōchihōkankei ni kansuru Shinriron no Mosaku," *Jichikenkyū* (January/February 1984), p. 54; Michio Muramatsu, "Sēfukankankei to Sējitaisei," in Ōmori Wataru and Satō Seizaburō, eds., *Nihon no Chihōsēfu* (Tokyo: Tokyo Daigaku Shuppankai, 1986).

2. Akira Amakawa, "Senryō to Chihōsēdo no Kaikaku," in Yoshikazu Sakamoto and R. E. Ward, eds., *Nihonsenryō no Kenkyū* (Tokyo: Tokyo Daigaku Shuppankai, 1987), p. 119 (my translation).

but also separation. According to Amakawa, the postwar center-local relationship has been one of combined decentralization and loose interfusion. As has been pointed out by those like Amakawa and Minoru Nakano the reality of the center-local relationship is that the area of local autonomy is rather large.[3]

Muramatsu says that the problem with the analysis until now is that it has ignored three points.[4] First is that the center-local relationship is not only an administrative relationship but also a political relationship. Until now, it has been recognized only that local governments have used politics to put pressure on the central government. The second point is that local governments make fewer decisions based on direction from the central government than heretofore recognized and, in fact, a large part of local government activity is autonomous. The third point is that local government decisions are often influenced by local general elections and competition with other local governments.

Based on quantitative analysis, the economist Takerō Doi states the following: "[A]s a whole, local finance is rather institutionally centralized, particularly with regard to revenue; however, administratively, local governments can use their discretion in a limited way."[5]

If one looks at several sets of data, some decentralization is apparent. Table 9-1 shows data for public construction projects (as of project start). When amounts for regional governments, local governments, and local public corporations are combined, the total accounts for around two-thirds of spending in the years shown and is far greater than the aggregate share for the central government, public corporations, and government corporations.

For a more general perspective, table 9-2 shows general government expenditure as a percentage of GDP. Japanese local and regional expenditure is four times national government expenditure and is a bit below that of the federated countries Germany and Canada; however, it is much higher than that of the United States, which is also a federated country. Japan stands out particularly for its large local public capital formation (gross fixed capital formation plus net purchase of land). The Japanese public construction state discussed in chapter 3 still exists with vigor in the twenty-first century.

3. Minoru Nakano, *Gendai Nihon no Seisaku Katei* (Tokyo: Tokyo Daigaku Shuppankai, 1992).

4. Muramatsu, "Sēfukankankei to Sējitaisei," in Wataru and Seizaburo, *Nihon no Chihōsēfu*, p. 145.

5. Takerō Doi, *Chihōzaisei no Sējikēzaigaku* (Tokyo: Tōyō Kēzai Shinbunsha, 2000), p. 247 (my translation).

Table 9-1. *Total Public Works Construction Expenditure at Start of Project, 1980–99*

					Project originated by			
Year	*Total*	*Central government*	*Public corporation*	*Government corporation*	*Regional government*	*Local government*	*Local public corporation*	*Other*
Expenditure (billions of yen)								
1980	11,439.6	1,279.0	1,013.3	1,418.2	3,182.8	3,180.1	882.0	484.1
1985	11,000.0	1,172.4	890.9	800.1	3,526.8	3,328.8	848.1	432.9
1990	14,604.6	1,673.4	1,402.0	379.0	4,684.2	4,924.5	936.4	604.9
1995	19,216.5	2,807.6	1,720.9	602.1	6,247.0	5,765.1	1,234.7	839.0
1999	15,372.3	2,823.4	1,534.4	479.9	4,734.0	4,105.3	1,076.2	619.0
Share of total (percent)								
1980		11.2	8.9	12.4	27.8	27.8	7.7	4.2
1985		10.7	8.1	7.3	32.1	30.3	7.7	3.9
1990		11.5	9.6	2.6	32.1	33.7	6.4	4.1
1995		14.6	9.0	3.1	32.5	30.0	6.4	4.4
1999		18.4	10.0	3.1	30.8	26.7	7.0	4.0

Source: Kensetsu Chōsa Tōkei Kenkyū Kai, *Kensetsu Tōkei Yōran* (Tokyo: Kensetsu Bukka Chōsakai, various years).

Table 9-2. *General Government Expenditure, Selected Countries*[a]
Percent of GDP

Country (local:national ratio)	Total	Public capital formation[b]	Consumption
Japan (80:20)			
Local government	12.9	5.6	7.4
National government	3.3	1.0	2.3
Total	16.2		
United States (66:34)			
Local government	11.2	1.8	9.5
National government	5.9	0.1	5.7
Total	17.1		
United Kingdom[c] (37:63)			
Local government	8.2	0.8	7.4
National government	14.0	0.6	13.4
Total	22.2		
France (42:58)			
Local government	7.5	2.0	5.5
National government	10.4	0.5	9.9
Total	17.9		
Germany (83:17)			
Local government[d]	11.3	1.7	9.7
National government	2.4	0.2	2.2
Total	13.7		
Italy[e] (51:49)			
Local government	9.1	1.6	7.5
National government	8.9	0.5	8.4
Total	18.0		
Canada (81:19)			
Local government[d]	18.0	1.9	16.1
National government	4.1	0.3	3.8
Total	22.1		

Source: *OECD National Accounts,* vol. 2, Detailed Tables (1960–97).
a. Excludes social security expenditures. Figures may not add, due to rounding.
b. Public capital formation = gross fixed capital formation + net purchase of land.
c. Data are for 1996.
d. Combines state and provincial government and local government figures.
e. Data are for 1995.

In spite of these data, many still contend that the central government financially controls local governments through local allocation tax (LAT) disbursements and other subsidies, that the central government uses finance as a lever, and that centralization is still strong.[6] These elements exist. However, the question is not whether the central government controls local governments or how strong that control is. The issue, as will be explained later, is whether the current local finance system blurs the responsibilities of the central and local governments and whether that creates moral hazard.

Tradition of Decentralization from the Edo Period

As was stated in chapters 2 and 7, it is appropriate to think that the tradition of power decentralization since the Edo period has continued, at least to the present, in spite of the Meiji Restoration and postwar reforms. Although the dissolution of the domains and the establishment of a new system of control through educational meritocracy by the Meiji Restoration led to the development of a certain degree of centralization, for the most part, the autonomous villages from the Edo period continued as they were. In this sense, the local governments had dual functions after the Meiji Restoration. In other words, the prefectures and cities, towns, and villages functioned under self-governance, while at the same time locally implementing central government administration. From the Amakawa point of view, the system had strong elements of interfusion, but from the point of view of centralization and decentralization, quite a bit of the decentralization element remained. It could be called a gentle system of centralization.

The question is how did the postwar reforms change the system that had been in place since the Meiji period and in what form has it survived to the present? Since the Ministry of the Interior was dissolved, the prewar local policy with the prefectural governor as the nexus had greatly changed and the centralized structure of the interior minister, governor, and mayor had collapsed.

---

6. The local allocation tax system is designed to equalize revenues among local governments and to maintain a standard level of public services. When local tax revenues are insufficient to cover the expenses of local governments for the provision of standard administrative services, the local allocation tax covers the shortage. The local allocation tax is allotted to local governments through the Special Account for Allotment of Local Allocation Tax and Transferred Tax.

"Because the Ministry of the Interior was dissolved with the recognition of the continuing existence of the dual functions of local self-governance, the control through direction and subsidies by central ministries remained," according to Amakawa, "and was directly tied to localities through individual laws with regard to particular tasks."[7] In this sense, Amakawa's element of interfusion has been maintained, albeit in a different form. To use Amakawa's terms, the gentle system of centralization and interfusion became a gentle system of decentralization and interfusion. According to his analysis, the dissolution of the Ministry of the Interior strengthened the influence of the Ministry of Finance and the budget (subsidies and local allocation tax disbursements) became more important.

It is true that the Ministry of Home Affairs, which was created after the Ministry of the Interior was dissolved, was in many ways the local finance ministry, and undoubtedly the Ministry of the Interior's direct authority was replaced with an indirect finance authority.[8] The Ministry of Home Affairs skillfully allied itself with the politicians and did not surrender to the power of the Ministry of Finance. Rather, the issue of local finance, such as the local allocation tax, became almost hallowed ground to the Ministry of Finance, and between the Ministry of Finance and the Ministry of Home Affairs there was a tacit understanding that the Ministry of Finance would not directly intervene in the budget process for local finance. What Amakawa has not revealed is that politicians were extremely powerful with regard to local finance and that the political power regularly rested with the Ministry of Home Affairs. In the context of the center versus local and the Ministry of Finance versus Ministry of Home Affairs dichotomy, most politicians were on the side of the Ministry of Home Affairs. Positioned as they were between the local groups and the Ministry of Home Affairs, the politicians often functioned as coordinators.

Post-Edo Party Politics and Local Benefits

The development of party politics since the Meiji period is closely related to local self-governance and local benefits. As a majority of important positions in the Meiji government were held by those who came from the Chōshū and Satsuma domains and as those who came from other domains and the

---

7. Amakawa, "Senryō to Chihōsēdo no Kaikaku," pp. 341–42 (my translation).
8. In January 2001, the name of the Ministry of Home Affairs was changed to the Ministry of Public Management, Home Affairs, Posts, and Telecommunications.

Edo government pursued political causes, such as liberal civil rights and the establishment of a parliament, these groups began to gradually form political parties with support in local areas. The continuation from the prewar to the postwar period of the opposition between the Satsuma-Chōshū-led government and political parties and the bureaucratic system and political parties combined to make a very Japanese structure. This structure was to become one of the facets of modern Japan, which had completed gentle centralization while maintaining the autonomous villages from the Edo period.[9] Nakano analyzed the channels for coordination of local benefits since the high growth period (figure 9-1) and found that local governments were acting autonomously and the involvement of politics had increased.[10] Of particular interest is the point that the real initiative for budget requests did not come from prefectural bureaucrats but for the most part from governors and politicians. He points out the increased involvement of politicians in the budget formation process, for example, as evidenced by the requests for increased subsidy rates for subsidized enterprises.[11]

In any case, since the Meiji period, political parties and politicians have become deeply involved in the disbursement of benefits to local areas and, as a result, party politics has grown stronger. Even in the public construction state formed after the war by Kakuei Tanaka, politicians and the Ministry of Home Affairs have played an important role. The problem is that the local finance system is now obsolete and local, as well as central, governments are nearly insolvent. Furthermore, because of this the local communities that have been the foundation of the country since the Edo period are about to collapse financially.

The Collapse of Local Finances

Tables 9-3 and 9-4 show the structure of local finance expenditure by purpose and type. Looking at the purpose for expenditure, the largest amount is for construction. When it is combined with public works–related public bonds, which make up a large part of "other expenditures," it becomes more than 30 percent of the total expenditure. Looking at the type of

9. For more on this issue, see Takashi Mikuriya, "Nihonsēji ni Okeru Chihōriekiron no Saikentō," *Leviathan,* vol. 2 (Spring 1988), pp. 141, 150; and Taisuke Ueda, *Saikyōsaishō: Hara Kei* (Tokyo: Tokuma Shoten, 1992), p. 3.

10. Nakano, *Gendai Nihon no Seisaku Katei,* pp. 229, 258.

11. Ibid., pp. 214, 218.

expenditure, when investment capital is combined with public bonds, the percentage is in the upper thirties or higher.

The point is that most expenditures, except for compulsory expenditures like personnel and welfare, go for public works and their financing. Regular construction projects are divided into central government–subsidized projects (44 percent of total construction in 1999), direct central government–controlled projects (9 percent) and independent projects (47 percent). The real central government burden is large not only in terms of central government–subsidized projects but also in terms of independent projects. This is because the central government subsidizes the local government through such measures as current-year and subsequent-year revisions of public works expenditures (they both come out of the central government's local allocation tax for local governments).

For a given government-subsidized (local) project the central government pays 50 percent directly, which means the local government could be expected to cover the remaining 50 percent. In reality, however, the central government subsidizes more than this amount, through the payment to the local government of subsidies financed through national taxes. For the local government's original 50 percent share of a given project, the central government pays two types of subsidies:

—It subsidizes 25 percent through a direct payment to the local government in the year the project is started.

—The local government is then permitted to issue local bonds to finance the remaining 75 percent of its responsibility for the project. The maturity of the bonds can vary but the local government must pay interest periodically and principal at maturity to bondholders. However, the central government pays a subsidy to the local government in an amount equal to 70 percent of the principal and interest that the local government must pay to bondholders over the life of the bond (that is, 0.7×75 percent = 52.5 percent).

As a result, the central government pays 25 percent plus 52.5 percent, leaving 22.5 percent as the local government's true share of its half of the project. Thus, for a given project, the central government pays 88.75 percent, leaving only 11.25 percent to be paid by the local government.[12]

Similarly, subsidies from the central to local government are paid for independent projects in which the local government could be expected to

12. Japan, Ministry of Finance data.

Figure 9-1. *Communication and Mediation Channels for Local Benefits*

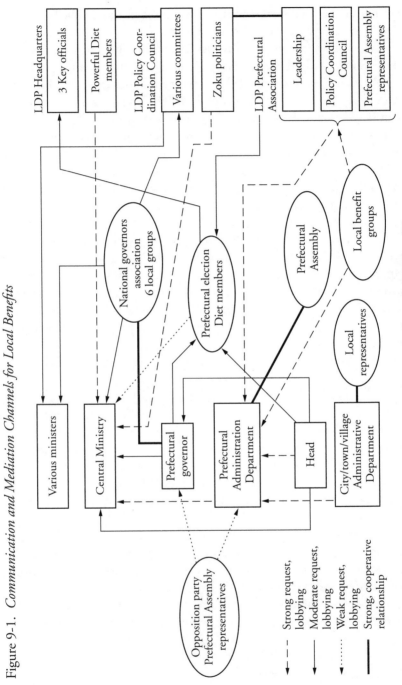

Source: Minoru Nakano, *Gendai Nihon no Seisaku Katei* (Tokyo: Tokyo Daigaku Shuppankai, 1992), p. 228.

Table 9-3. *Local Fiscal Expenditure, by Purpose, 1994–99*[a]

Percent

Expenditure	1994	1995	1996	1997	1998	1999
Assembly	0.6	0.6	0.6	0.6	0.6	0.6
General affairs	9.8	10.1	9.8	8.9	8.6	9.0
Public welfare	11.8	12.1	12.3	13.0	13.4	14.8
Public sanitation	6.8	6.5	6.7	6.9	6.6	6.5
Labor	0.6	0.5	0.5	0.5	0.5	0.6
Agriculture, fisheries, and forestry	6.8	6.9	6.9	6.6	6.4	6.1
Commerce and industry	5.7	5.7	5.4	5.5	6.2	5.9
Construction	23.1	23.3	22.7	21.8	21.9	20.6
Police and fire	5.2	5.2	5.3	5.4	5.3	5.2
Education	19.8	18.9	19.0	19.2	18.6	17.9
Other[b]	9.7	10.2	10.8	11.6	11.9	12.7

Source: Data through 1998 are from *Chihō Zaisei Yōran* (Chihō Zaimu Kyōkai, 2000). Data for 1999 are from *Chihō Zaisei Hakusho* (Ministry of Finance, 2001).

a. All figures are from finalized accounts based on normal accounting procedures. Duplications have been eliminated from provincial and local figures. Columns may not add to 100, due to rounding.

b. Includes public bonds.

Table 9-4. *Local Fiscal Expenditure, by Type, 1994–99*[a]

Percent

Expenditure	1994	1995	1996	1997	1998	1999
Obligatory	41.1	40.4	42.1	44.4	44.4	45.0
Personnel	26.9	26.1	26.7	27.6	27.0	26.6
Aid	5.6	5.6	5.8	6.3	6.5	6.8
Public bonds	8.6	8.7	9.5	10.5	10.8	11.6
Investment	32.0	32.5	31.0	28.9	28.8	26.4
Normal construction	31.2	31.4	30.2	28.9	28.2	25.7
Supplementary works	11.9	12.7	12.0	11.3	11.9	11.5
Independent works	18.2	17.3	16.9	15.8	14.6	12.7
Disaster recovery works	0.7	1.0	0.8	0.5	0.5	0.7
Unemployment works	0.1	0.1	0.0	0.0	0.0	0.0
Other	26.9	27.1	26.9	26.7	26.8	28.6

Source: See table 9-2.

a. All figures are from finalized accounts based on normal accounting procedures. Duplications have been eliminated from provincial and local figures. Columns may not add to 100, due to rounding.

cover 100 percent of costs. For these projects, the central government actually finances 56.25 percent through subsidies, leaving 43.75 percent to be paid directly by the local government.[13]

In reality, it is possible to see that the system is such that the central government finances most local construction, and because of this, there is inefficiency. It is also the reason public works that are of little benefit to the local areas are allowed to continue without being scaled down. Moral hazard is built into the system. Considering the system that has been created, it would not be surprising that local governments and citizens believe public works to be justified because of the jobs and income they create. However, recently even local governments have objected to public works because of concerns about environmental problems and financial collapse. Even if the central government agrees to bear a substantial part of the financial burden, the local government still bears some financial responsibility. Although the projects do create jobs and income, this may be disproportionately more beneficial to the construction companies than to the local community.

The moral hazard problem exists not only for public expenditures, such as public construction, but also for mandatory spending. This is mainly because the standards for calculating the LAT disbursement for local governments are not clear.[14] Many think that if the local government worked hard to lower its expenditures, this would serve only to decrease the disbursement of the LAT from the central government. Meanwhile, if their expenditures increase, the LAT disbursement would also increase. The amount of the regular local allocation tax is calculated as standard revenues subtracted from standard financial demand.[15] If the standard revenues are

13. Ministry of Home Affairs, *Chihō Zaisei no Shikumi to sono Unei no Jittai* (Chihō Zaimu Kyōkai, 1996), p 379.

14. The total local allocation tax is broken down into the special allocation tax (6 percent of the total LAT), which is used to meet special or extraordinary financial needs (for example, natural disasters), and the regular (also called "ordinary") allocation tax (94 percent) used to cover standard financial resource shortages.

15. Annually, the national government estimates the expenditures and revenues of all local governments, and these are then consolidated into the Local Financial Plan. Expenditures are estimated as the standard financial demand, which should represent general financial resources that are required to provide standard levels of administrative services based on reasonable standards. Its calculation takes into account local natural, geographical, and social conditions such as population size and area size, but other adjustment factors are also included and these factors are numerous, arbitrarily derived, and nontransparent. Like the standard financial demand, standard revenues are calculated each year for local governments. However, unlike the demand figures, revenue figures are based on a percentage of past

insufficient to cover the standard financial demand for a particular local government, the regular local allocation tax is allotted to that government in line with the level of the shortage.

The problem is that the calculation of the standard financial demand is arbitrary and nontransparent. The standard financial demand is calculated by multiplying the unit cost (based on standard conditions for providing a standard administrative service) by the quantitative measure for each administrative service (for example, number of teachers and students for education) by an adjustment coefficient. However, it is not clear how the adjustment coefficient is calculated. It is supposed to reflect adjustments for special regional characteristics that are not reflected in either the unit cost or quantitative measure, but there is a significant possibility that the standard financial demand is being decided in an arbitrary or political manner by manipulating the adjustment coefficient. This being the case, it would not be surprising if there were local governments that thought it would be better to move politically to increase the amount of disbursement from the central government rather than have administrative reform.[16]

Collapse of the Special Account for the Local Allocation Tax

In this way, the local allocation tax system was a type of buffer for local governments, and because of that buffer the local government expenditure for public construction increased to the point where it surpassed ¥100 trillion in 1998. It was the Special Account for the Allotment of Local Allocation Tax and Local Transferred Tax (hereinafter, the Local Allocation Tax Special Account) that stood between the central government's general account and local governments and played an important role in local finance.

The high level of local government funding by disbursements from the Local Allocation Tax Special Account is evident in the calculation of the LAT for fiscal year 2001. Outstanding borrowings in the Local Allocation

---

local tax revenues and the local transferred tax. Therefore, the standard revenues are more transparent and less arbitrary than the standard financial demand.

16. Further information (in English) on the local allocation tax and local public finance in general can be obtained from the following: Japan, Ministry of Public Management, Home Affairs, Posts and Telecommunications, "White Paper on Local Public Finance, 2002"; Japan, Cabinet Office, "Annual Report on Japan's Economy and Public Finance, 2000–2001," December 2001; and Japan, Ministry of Finance, Budget Bureau, "The Japanese Budget in Brief, 2001," www.mof.go.jp/English/budget/brief/2001/brief15.htm [August 2003].

Tax Special Account for FY2001 totaled ¥43.4 trillion. The difference between this amount and the repayment amount of ¥38.8 trillion was passed along to the local level as the local allocation tax disbursement. In FY2001, more than 70 percent of the revenue in the Local Allocation Tax Special Account was made up of borrowed funds. Since the special account was originally intended to be composed of special funds or special annual revenue, the fact that more than 70 percent of annual revenue is borrowed means that this special account has failed. Most of this borrowed money is dealt with by short-term loans from the Trust Fund Bureau. As of the end of FY2000, the amount of lending from the Trust Fund Bureau was ¥32.1 trillion and, in fact, 94 percent of that, or ¥30 trillion, was in the form of lending to the Local Allocation Tax Special Account.

In the Local Financial Plan, after the local allocation tax disbursement, the national Treasury disbursement is the next largest source of revenue and has increased to an extraordinary ¥13.1 trillion.[17] This includes various subsidies from the central government to local areas. Table 9-5 shows the sum of these subsidies to local governments along with other items for FY2000 to FY2004 in the *Midterm Look at Finances*.

In FY2001, the combined sum of the local allocation tax and the subsidy to local governments amounted to ¥34.1 trillion, and this is more than the ¥31.4 trillion left over when the subsidy to local governments is subtracted from general expenditures. Except for the funds that service the national debt, over half of the central government's annual revenue goes to local governments. This means that the annual expenditure for local governments is the reason for more than half of the central government's national debt and, someday, this must be paid out of the general account. When this is viewed in conjunction with the problem of short-term lending by the Trust Fund Bureau, which was over ¥30 trillion to the Local Allocation Tax Special Account in FY2001, it becomes clear that an important part of consolidating central government public finances is related to local government expenditures. As was shown in table 9-2, 80 percent of Japan's general government expenditure is made up of local expenditures. In this respect, it can be deduced that local expenditures contribute to 80 percent of the fiscal deficit.

---

17. Revenue sources in the Local Financial Plan include local taxes, the local allocation tax, the national Treasury disbursement, and local government bonds, among others.

Table 9-5. *The Midterm Look at Finances*[a]

Expenditure	2000	2001	2002	2003	2004
National bonds					
Percent change		−21.8	7.1	6.2	6.3
Trillions of yen	22.0	17.2	18.4	19.5	20.8
Local allocation tax (LAT)					
Percent change		12.7	15.6	1.3	6.9
Trillions of yen	14.9	16.8	19.5	19.7	21.1
General					
Percent change		1.2	1.6	1.6	2.2
Trillions of yen	48.1	48.7	49.5	50.2	51.3
Corporate guarantees					
Percent change		4.7	5.1	4.2	4.2
Trillions of yen	16.8	17.6	18.4	19.2	20.0
Public works					
Percent change		0.0	0.0	0.1	0.2
Trillions of yen	9.4	9.4	9.4	9.4	9.5
Other					
Percent change		−1.0	−0.4	0.0	1.2
Trillions of yen	21.9	21.7	21.6	21.6	21.8
Local government subsidies[b]					
Percent change		2.8	0.0	0.0	0.0
Trillions of yen	16.9	17.3	17.3	17.3	17.3
Total					
Percent change		−2.7	5.6	2.5	4.1
Trillions of yen	85.0	82.7	87.3	89.5	93.2

Source: Japan, Ministry of Finance, *Zaisei no Chūki Tenbō* (various issues).

a. The *Midterm Look at Finances* projects the finance situation through 2004, based on the previous year's burden estimates and the systems and policies of 2001 and assuming real economic growth of 2 percent and 0 percent change in the consumer price index. Furthermore, it assumes that the investment element of general expenditure will be the same as that of the previous year.

b. Estimate; not included in the *Midterm Look at Finances*. Since the estimate does not take into account policy changes with regard to aid money, in principle this is driven by price increases.

Gentle Decentralization and Gentle Separation of Power

The remainder of this chapter summarizes the analysis thus far and explores a new direction for reform. First, thinking of Japan as a simple centralized state is an extreme ideological position and such an interpretation will lead to misunderstanding. It is also clear that simply transferring authority from the center to the local areas would be naïve. Such conceptualization of decentralization is meaningless. It has also been pointed out that the problem is not only the administrative system, but also, importantly, the political system.

It seems that the local administrative system, of which the LAT and subsidies such as the National Treasury outlay are a part, is at the center of the complex central-local and administrative-political mechanisms. Of particular importance is the extremely arbitrary and political system that is currently in place and that has created a moral hazard problem. This has led to the enormous fiscal deficit. The arbitrary finance and political systems are the result of compromises made in the discord between Japan's central government and political parties since the Meiji period. The effect of this system is the loss of efficiency in the public sector and the loss of discipline in government finance.

One of the solutions that has been proposed is to move the funds directly to the local areas, or in other words, to dissolve the LAT system and change the national tax to a local tax. If this were realistically possible, it would solve the moral hazard problem. However, this plan will not work in reality because companies are centered in large cities like Tokyo and many of the local areas have become depopulated. As long as Japan is one nation, even if it were to become a federation, it would be impossible to materially shrink public services in areas such as Miyagi, Shimane, and Ishikawa prefectures, which have no prospects for annual revenue, and at the same time to materially increase public services or drastically reduce taxes in cities like Tokyo. In fact, table 9-6 shows that the percentage of local tax revenue is already very high at 41 percent for a nonfederated state and is not low even when compared to that of federated states, such as the United States and Australia.

Furthermore, even if the details of local finance could be amended, it would be difficult to change the total amount of tax transfers from the present level. In this situation, the tax transfer itself cannot be changed much, and the question becomes: what reforms, in the form of transfers, can be implemented?

First, with regard to the LAT and its funds, the details should be made transparent. It is important to make sure that the details cannot be changed by politics or by the arbitrariness of administration. In some way, an indicator needs to be created to estimate the efficiency of expenditure and that should be linked to the LAT disbursement.

Table 9-6. *Central and Local Government Tax Revenue Share in Selected Countries, 1965–99*

Percent of total

Country	Central government	Local government
Federated		
Australia	78.5	21.5
Canada	47.6	52.4
Germany	49.5	50.5
Switzerland	46.7	53.3
United States	59.1	40.9
Centralized government		
France	80.4	19.6
England	95.2	4.8
Japan	58.8	41.2

Source: Mikiko Iwasaki, "Chiho Kofuzei to Hojokin wo Meguru Seijigaku," *Revaiasan,* vol. 6 (Spring 1990), p. 54. Data compiled from OECD, *Revenue Statistics of OECD Countries* (Paris, 1965–99).

Local allocation tax systems should take into account the experiences of progressive local governments and they should not create a moral hazard problem. In order to rebuild the government finance structure, decreasing local expenditure is indispensable, and to accomplish that, the total amount of LAT disbursement and subsidies from the central government must be decreased. It is also necessary, however, to change the structure itself. It will be particularly important to reform the mechanism in cooperation with progressive local governments in depopulated areas.

The subsidy for independent projects should be decreased as much as possible and should be shifted to the general subsidy. For example, public works should be essentially independent regional projects or under the direct control of the central government, and subsidized projects should be only rare exceptions. Giving an additional subsidy to public works by using the LAT, for example, should be abolished. The influence of the central ministries over local governments through subsidies should not be maintained. If it is necessary to have the central government carry out the projects, in many cases, it may be preferable to have the central government take direct control. While I do not advocate the cessation of all delegation, if there is too much of what Amakawa calls interfusion, the moral hazard problem is inevitable. Gentle decentralization and gentle separation of power is desirable in local administration and local finance for the future.

The root of this problem, centralization of everything in Tokyo, runs quite deep, however. As has been explained before, the Meiji Restoration created a capital in Tokyo as the center of the new nation free from legacies of the past, while at the same time maintaining autonomous villages. Because of this, Tokyo has played an extremely important and unique role in the process of Japan's modernization. The intense central concentration is for the most part a result of this movement. In order to disperse this central concentration, the cities and towns, which were once castle cities, need to be revitalized. For this, the cities and towns must, like Tokyo, be more open and receptive to newcomers.[18] It would be desirable for villages to maintain their traditions and culture while at the same time adapting to the times by becoming more open. If they remain closed, however, they will only continue to be depopulated.

Local governments must also work to attract private companies, particularly headquarters of large corporations. In addition to providing various financial benefits, the local governments must create areas where it is comfortable for salaried workers, and even foreigners, to live. With plentiful attractions, such as nature, land, and traditional culture, it should be possible to rebuild cities and towns and local culture, as they existed during the Edo period.

18. Local communities in Japan tend to be very parochial and to discriminate against outsiders in subtle ways. This is particularly true of older communities.

10 Fundamental Change in Agricultural Policy

The agricultural revolution took place between 1600 and 1720, and during that time the population increased from 10 million to 30 million, while agricultural productivity grew an estimated 300 percent. In contrast with Great Britain's industrial revolution, Akira Hayami calls this the "industrious" revolution.[1]

The traditional agricultural methods established during the middle of the Edo period were highly productive and supported Japan during the Meiji Restoration as it moved toward modernization and industrialization. Shinzaburō Ōishi states that viewed from any angle, the Tokugawa system was a substantive and unique civilization with vitality and originality.[2] Although agricultural productivity increased further with the Meiji Agriculture Method created around 1888, Japan at the end of the Edo period and the

1. Akira Hayami, "Kinsenihon no Hatten to Industrious Revolution," in Akira Hayami, Osamu Saito, and Shinya Sugiyama, eds., *Tokugawashakai karano Tembō-Hatten, Kōzō, Kokusaikankei* (Tokyo: Dobunkan-shuppan, 1989).
2. Shinzaburō Ōishi, *Edojidai to Kindaika* (Tokyo: Chikumashobō, 1986).

beginning of the Meiji period could be viewed as an extremely advanced agricultural state. Using the *tsubokarichō*, or land yield records, for analysis, Tsuneo Sato and Shinzaburō Ōishi comment as follows:[3]

> Though it cannot be denied that the third decade of Meiji was certainly a turning point for Japanese rice productivity, this does not mean that there was a distinct difference in level compared with that produced under the previous agricultural method used from the middle of the Edo period to the second decade of Meiji. During the third decade of Meiji, the yield per [unit of land] had fallen in some areas . . . in the third phase at the beginning of Showa, there was for some a big increase in rice productivity . . . there are more than a few examples showing that land yields from the middle of Edo until the war were at almost the same level.
>
> It should not be hastily decided that the agricultural productivity level under the traditional agricultural method used since the middle of the Edo period is necessarily lower in comparison with that of modern agriculture or prewar Japanese agriculture. The necessary elements for robust analysis of productivity levels of traditional agricultural methods are indicated in the tsubokarichō.[4]

Table 10-1 shows the productivity of rice cultivation and land yield by harvest area. It becomes clear that, even with some change at the turn of the century, the structure of Japanese agriculture had not altered very much from the middle of Edo period until the mid-1950s. In 1950, there were 6.18 million farm households and 16.36 million farmers—17 percent of those households used only manpower, 26 percent used man and animal power, 48 percent used man and animal power combined with machines, and 9 percent used manpower and machines. While there have been some changes, for the most part, much has stayed the same since the Edo period.

Even from the turn of the century, the agricultural population was around 15 million, agricultural land was about 6 million *chōbu*, and there were about 5.5 million farm households.[5] Thus, the basic structure of agriculture has remained essentially stable in spite of some variation.

3. *Tsubokarichō* are continuous records of land yields that were kept by the village.
4. Tsuneo Sato and Shinzaburō Ōishi, *Hinnōshikan o Minaosu* (Tokyo: Kōdansha Gendaishinsho, 1995), pp. 85, 87 (my translation).
5. One *chōbu* is equal to approximately 10,000 square meters, or one hectare.

Origins of Landownership

What changed during the Meiji and subsequent periods (to the 1950s) was the relationship between landlord and farmer. The land reform between 1873 and 1881 changed land tax from payment in kind to money, as described in chapter 2. And because the government officially recognized landlords (that is, landowners who did not farm their own land), the number of tenant farmers and the proportion of tenant farmland dramatically increased.[6] In 1872, before land tax reform, tenant farmers were 29 percent; by 1892, that share had jumped to 40 percent, and by 1940, to 45 percent.

From the Taisho to Showa period, as farmers frequently rioted, farm villages became poor, social and political problems developed and the government gradually began to favor independent farming. In line with this, an alliance was formed between the progressive bureaucrats and the military. Passage of two laws, the Farmland Adjustment Law in 1938 and the Food Control Law in 1942, resulted in the weakening of the power of landlords and the expansion of the power of small, independent farmers.

Ironically, this reform movement, which was begun by the new reform-minded bureaucrats, was completed under the General Headquarters (GHQ) after World War II.[7] Under the 1946 Second Land Reform Bill, farmland that belonged to nonresident landlords in cities, towns, and villages and farms that were more than one hectare (four hectares in Hokkaido) were to be sold. By around 1950, 80 percent of tenant farmland was free and was occupied by small-scale, independent farmers. Then at the request of the GHQ, the Agricultural Land Law was enacted in 1952 with the goal of making sure that the landlord system could not be revived. Under this law the acquisition of land by those other than farmers was prohibited and the conversion of farmland was severely restricted. It is in this context that independent farming was established and farming was combined with ownership, management, and labor. Article 1 of the Agricultural Land Law "recognizes as most appropriate, the ownership of farmland by the farmer himself and promotes the ownership of farmland by the farmer and supports that right . . . with that, it holds as its objective the

6. In the Edo era there were no landlords who did not farm their own land.

7. The full name is General Headquarters (GHQ) of the Supreme Commander for the Allied Powers (SCAP); the SCAP was General Douglas MacArthur.

Table 10-1. *Rice Productivity and Land Yield, by Harvest Area, 1809–Present*

Harvest area[a]	Record	Yield[b]	Up to 1898	1899–1927	1928–57	1958–77
					Period	
Kai no Kuni	1877–present	Yield per tsubo (sho)	1.35	1.36	1.79	2.43
Koma-gun		Standard deviation (sho)	0.246	0.257	0.340	0.368
Kamisasao-mura		Coefficient of variation	0.182	0.189	0.190	0.151
Kai no Kuni	1862–present	Yield per tsubo (sho)	1.70	1.77	1.89	2.42
Koma-gun		Standard deviation (sho)	0.276	0.325	0.395	0.340
Shibusawa-mura		Coefficient of variation	0.162	0.183	0.209	0.140
Kai no Kuni	1816–1974	Yield per tsubo (sho)	1.37	1.94	1.98	2.63
Koma-gun		Standard deviation (sho)	0.371	0.350	0.432	0.245
Nagasaka Kamijo-mura		Coefficient of variation	0.271	0.180	0.218	0.093
Ise no Kuni	1809–present	Yield per tsubo (sho)	1.23	1.47	1.64	2.24
Tagata-gun		Standard deviation (sho)	0.236	0.284	0.321	0.265
Koike-mura		Coefficient of variation	0.192	0.193	0.196	0.118
Shinano no Kuni	1817–present	Yield per tsubo (sho)	1.64	1.91	2.11	1.96
Kambara-gun		Standard deviation (sho)	0.234	0.188	0.199	0.262
Hachiman-mura		Coefficient of variation	0.142	0.098	0.095	0.134
Kai no Kuni	1812–present	Yield per tsubo (sho)	1.49	1.46	1.87	2.88
Koma-gun		Standard deviation (sho)	0.383	0.232	0.335	0.430
Shimowano-mura		Coefficient of variation	0.257	0.159	0.179	0.149

Source: Tsuneo Sata and Shinzaburo Ōishi, *Hinnō Shikan o Minaosu* (Tokyo: Kōdansha Gendai Shinsho, 1995), p. 86.

a. *Kuni* refers to a domain; *gun* is the equivalent of a county; *mura* is a village.

b. *Tsubo* is a measure equal to 3.3 meters. *Sho* is a measure equal to 1.8 liters.

stabilization of the status of farmers and progress in farm productivity."[8] This article continues to govern today in spite of the changes in agricultural policy, the enactment of numerous new laws, and the revision of laws since the 1950s. In other words, independent farming has continued to be a core principle of postwar agricultural policy. As will be explained later, this idealistic notion of independent farming has obstructed true reform in Japanese agricultural policy and has been the most significant hindrance to agriculture efficiency.

Agricultural Structural Reform and Administration

The structure of Japanese agriculture was reshaped during the high growth period. In 1955 there were 15.06 million farmers, which amounts to 38 percent of the total 39.59 million employed. Japan still seemed very much like an agricultural nation. Table 10-2 illustrates how, with the high growth process, the farming population had fallen to 6.69 million in 1975, and by 2000, to 2.97 million, or 4.6 percent of total employment.

In 1985 Makoto Hata, who at the time was Director General of the Bureau of Structural Reform in the Ministry of Agriculture and Forestry (currently the Ministry of Agriculture, Forestry, and Fisheries), stated the following with regard to structural change:

> The agricultural population, which had not changed much from Meiji to the mid-1950s, has started to decrease dramatically. And, today, it has in fact reached one third, or 4.5 million. Furthermore, if we look at the key farming population that is under 60 years of age in the farm census, what was 9.98 million in [1960] had become 2.74 million by [1984], a dramatic decrease to 27.5 percent . . . in this way, the farmland per person of the employed population, "the ratio of people to land," has changed greatly; in addition, the important change is that the nature of the 4.38 million farm households has changed remarkably. First, there is a separation between those who are dedicated to farming exclusively (full-time farmer) and those who are devoted to professions other than farming (part-time farmer); second, of those who are dedicated exclusively to farming, there are some who are trying to shift their core products to such

---

8. Agricultural Land Law (my translation).

Table 10-2. *Employment, by Sector*
Millions, except as indicated

Year	Total employed	Agriculture		Construction		Manufacturing		Tertiary sector			
								Total		Food and beverage	
		Number	Percent	Number	Percent	Number	Percent	Number	Percent	Number	Percent
1904	26.02	15.67	60.2								
1915	27.23	14.95	54.9								
1925	28.44	13.32	46.8								
1935	31.40	13.36	42.5								
1941	32.58	13.62	41.8								
1947	33.33	16.62	49.9								
1950	36.02	16.36	45.4	1.54	4.3	5.70	15.8	10.67	29.6	3.99	11.1
1955	39.59	15.06	38.0	1.80	4.5	6.91	17.5	14.05	35.5	5.51	13.9
1960	44.04	13.27	30.1	2.69	6.1	9.57	21.7	16.84	38.2	6.98	15.8
1965	47.96	10.99	22.9	3.06	6.4	11.72	24.4	20.97	43.7	8.55	17.8
1970	52.59	9.40	17.9	3.96	7.5	13.72	26.1	24.51	46.6	10.14	19.3
1975	53.14	6.69	12.6	4.73	8.9	13.25	24.9	27.52	51.8	11.37	21.4
1980	55.81	5.47	9.8	5.38	9.6	13.25	23.7	30.91	55.4	12.73	22.8
1985	58.36	4.85	8.3	5.27	9.0	13.97	23.9	33.44	57.3	13.38	22.9
1990	61.68	3.92	6.4	5.84	9.5	14.64	23.7	36.42	59.0	13.80	22.4
1995	64.14	3.43	5.3	6.63	10.3	13.56	21.1	39.64	61.8	14.62	22.8
2000	64.46	2.97	4.6	6.53	10.1	13.21	20.5	41.42	64.3	14.74	22.9

Source: Compiled from Makoto Hata, *Nihon Nōgyōono Henbō–Nōogyōkizōmondai Nyūmon* (Tokyo: Nōgyōo Shinōchikai Chōsakai, 1985), pp. 22–23.

Table 10-3. *Full-Time and Part-Time Farm Households*[a]

Year	Total farm households (thousands)	Farm households that sell their products (thousands)	Full-time (percent)	Part-time (percent)	Part-time farm households (percent) Type 1[b]	Type 2[c]
1904	5,417					
1915	5,451		68.8	31.2		
1925	5,549		69.9	30.1		
1935	5,611		74.2	25.8		
1941	5,499		41.9	58.1	37.1	21.0
1947	5,909		55.4	44.6	28.5	16.1
1955	6,043		34.8	65.2	37.6	27.5
1965	5,665		21.5	78.5	36.7	41.7
1975	4,953		12.4	88.3	26.1	62.1
1985	4,229	3,315	15.0	84.9	22.9	62.1
1990	3,835	2,971	15.9	84.1	17.5	66.5
1995	3,444	2,651	16.1	83.9	18.8	65.1
2000	3,120	2,337	18.2	81.8	15.0	66.8

Source: Compiled from Hata, *Nihon Nōgyōono Henbō-Nōogyokōzōmondai Nyūmon*, pp. 22–23; and data from the Ministry of Public Management, Home Affairs, Posts, and Telecommunications.

a. Part-time farm households have at least one member with outside employment. Due to a change in method of calculation, full- and part-time percentages apply to "total farm households" for 1904–75, but to "farm households that sell their products" for 1985–2000.

b. Type 1 = Households with more than one member with outside employment and agricultural income greater than part-time external income.

c. Type 2 = Households with more than one member with outside employment generating income greater than agricultural income.

things as rice and wheat or dairy farming, which are dependent on large amounts of land, and others who are concentrating their management on efforts that conserve land such as landscape nursery, chicken farming, and pig farming. The appearance of these two divisions is at the base of the "transfiguration of Japanese agriculture."[9]

Table 10-3 shows the change in farm households from full-time to part-time. The Basic Agriculture Law of 1971 was enacted in response to the "transfiguration of agriculture" mentioned by Hata. With this, the Ministry

9. Makoto Hata, *Nihon Nōgyō no Henbō-Nōgyōkōzō Mondai Nyūmon* (Tokyo: Nōgyō Shinkōchiiki Chōsakai, 1985), pp. 27–29 (my translation).

of Agriculture, Forestry, and Fisheries directed policy toward the structural reform, modernization, and rationalization of agriculture as an industry. Incidentally, from 1960 to 1986, 261 laws and ordinances were enacted to reorganize the bureaucracy for the new framework of general agriculture administration and for structural reform of agriculture administration.

The main goal of the Basic Agriculture Law was to increase agricultural productivity and to address the income gap between the manufacturing and agricultural industries. For that, the objectives were a selective increase in agricultural production, price stability, and agriculture structural reform. However, this rationalization of agriculture and structural reform policy was based on top-down plans that focused on price controls and public works, and, because of that, it was very socialistic and leaned heavily toward agriculture cooperatives. Since it was rationalization and structural reform based on independent farming under the Agricultural Land Law, the average size of general farm households did not increase much. In fact, since 1975 abandoned fallow land has increased due to a reduction in farmland (table 10-4).

As is well known, the Food Control Law played an important part through price control in dissolving the income differential between manufacturing and agriculture. Under this law enacted in 1942, the government completely managed the distribution of rice, wheat, and soybeans. It was revised in 1952 and 1960 to make the price of rice fluctuate with wages in the cities and to guarantee income to farm households.

The Basic Agriculture Law's goal of eliminating income disparity between the manufacturing and agricultural industries was accomplished through the increase in income that was guaranteed under the Food Control Law. And in 1998 the average farm household's income rose to ¥8.68 million, which is much more than the ¥7.07 million of an average non–farm worker's household. Ironically, the fact that farm households surpassed non–farm households in average income was not due to the rationalization of agriculture or to structural adjustment, but was due to the rapidly increasing number of households that had part-time jobs in addition to farming and to measures like public works and price supports. In fact, the income of farm households that is derived strictly from agriculture is only 15 percent of the total average farm income of ¥8.68 million, or ¥1.25 million.

This reversal in the income differential was reflected in the assets and liabilities of these two sectors as well. Though the data are a bit old, the aver-

Table 10-4. *Fallow Land*

Year	Total fallow land (million ha)	Average landholding of farm households	Abandoned fallow land (million ha)
1904	5.25	0.97	
1915	5.81	1.07	
1925	6.02	1.08	
1935	6.01	1.07	
1941	5.81	1.06	
1947	5.24	0.89	
1955	5.14	0.86	
1965	6.00	0.91	
1975	5.57	0.97	0.10
1985	5.38	1.07	0.09
1995	5.04	1.20	0.16
2000	4.83	1.25	0.21

Source: See table 10-3.

age savings of a farm household in 1994 was ¥29.8 million, which was 2.4 times that of a non–farm worker's household. On the other hand, the average debt for a farm household was ¥3.27 million, which was only 47 percent of that of a non–farm worker's household.

Reality of Japanese Agriculture and the Collapse of Agricultural Policy

In 1999 the nominal gross domestic product of Japan's agriculture, forestry, and fisheries industry was ¥8.2 trillion, which was 1.7 percent of total GDP. This is nearly the same as for imports of agriculture, forestry, and fishery products, which totaled ¥7.8 trillion in 1998. What is important to note is that the total budget for the Ministry of Agriculture, Forestry, and Fisheries for the central and local governments of ¥9.8 trillion (the relevant central government budget was ¥3.4 trillion in 2000, and the local government budget was ¥6.2 trillion in 1999) was higher than the industry's GDP. Much of the agriculture budget went toward productivity measures (that is, measures to maintain the foundation of agricultural productivity such as irrigation, land reclamation, and farmland development) and reform of the structure of agriculture. These two types of measures accounted for 75 percent of the ministry's budget in 1999. Because of this, an unusual situation developed in which the budget for increasing total production and improving productivity was more than total production in agriculture and fisheries. In reality the ministry is using its budget for projects that do not contribute much to total agriculture or fisheries production. There are no figures for how much irrigation, land reclamation, and farmland development measures are increasing agricultural output; nevertheless agricultural production continues to decrease.

This strange relationship between agricultural production and the ministry budget can be seen in the numbers of farm households, agriculture cooperatives, and ministry employees. According to the 2000 agriculture census, the number of full-time farm households was 426,000,[10] the number of employees in agriculture cooperatives was 320,000 (1998), and the number of employees in the Ministry of Agriculture was 42,000 (2000). When the number of employees who work in ministry related public entities, in public enterprises, and in public corporations is added to the employees at the ministry and in cooperatives, the figure is just below 400,000. The total sum of employees in cooperatives and government is about the same as the number of full-time farm households. Relative to the number of people who are directly involved in agriculture production, there are far too many people who work on its administration and in the cooperatives.

These figures show how far Japanese agriculture has drifted from its basic function of production and how it is influenced by such factors as employment, income adjustment, politics, administration, and the budget. As a result, Japanese agriculture, compared to that of other developed countries, is in a very poor state as an industry. Of the Group of Five (G-5) countries, Japan has the highest percentage of farmers (4.5 percent); the United Kingdom has the lowest at 1.5 percent. The United States, which is an advanced agricultural nation, has 4 percent and France has 3.7 percent. Of course, most Japanese farm households are part-time.

In 1997, the portion of the U.S. federal budget that was agriculture related, excluding funding for food stamps, was approximately 1 percent. Compared to this, the portion of the general budget that is allocated to agriculture and fisheries in Japan is 3.3 percent, or three times that of the United States. In Japan's case, because national debt and local subsidies are much higher, if the analysis were done with general expenditures rather than with the total general budget, the budget share for agriculture and

10. Farm households "that sell their products"; see table 10-3, above.

fisheries would rise to 6.3 percent. In fact, this means that the share of the budget for agriculture, forestry, and fisheries in Japan is four to five times that of the advanced agricultural nation, the United States.

Even with this farm population and government subsidization, the ratio of Japan's domestic grain production to its grain consumption is the lowest of the G-5 countries at 27 percent (1998). As grain exporters, the United States's ratio is 135 percent (1997) and the United Kingdom's is 116 percent (1997).

What has caused this disaster? The answer is very clear. It is because agricultural administration is extremely politicized. The objective of administration was neither the nurture nor the promotion of the efficiency of agriculture as an industry; instead, it was the increase of employment in local towns and villages and the dissolution of the income differential between industries. Though the Food Control Law was enacted to eliminate the income gap, because of that the deficit in the Food Control Special Account at one point rose to ¥1.733 trillion (1979). Even now, 15 percent of the agriculture budget is for programs under the price and distribution policy.

Although the justification for this situation was the maintenance of an agricultural base, even the main functions of irrigation, land reclamation, and farmland development were for the creation of employment and income. Even now, despite approximately half of the agriculture budget being allotted to the maintenance of the agricultural base, no explanation is given for such a high level of public works spending for agriculture as an industry. There is an "iron triangle" among the Management Bureau of the Ministry of Agriculture, Forestry, and Fisheries; the LDP's Agriculture, Forestry, and Fisheries Committee and General Agriculture Administration Research Group; and vested interest groups (for example, the Irrigation Association). The argument that many projects are continued in order to protect the rights of vested interests seems to be convincing. There is social and political value to the elimination of the income gap and to increasing employment and income. In particular, the agriculture and fisheries administration has played more than a small role in the smooth progress of structural reform from agriculture to manufacturing without creating massive social and political upheaval. It did not, however, develop agriculture as an industry. Agricultural policy was the equivalent of employment and income policy for farm villages. With the end of high growth, that role has greatly diminished. Now, the system that was created by the politicians and bureaucrats to deal with agriculture has become a large burden for Japan and even for the agricultural villages themselves.

Revival of Agriculture as an Industry

Politics and administration did not, it must be acknowledged, stand idly by while the agriculture industry deteriorated and agricultural administration broke down. The administration attempted to address the issues through the implementation of new measures, but these were not effective. In 1995, the Food Supply Law was enacted to replace the Food Control Law; in 1993, a new system was established in response to the Uruguay Round Agriculture Agreement; and in 1999, the Basic Law on Food, Agriculture and Rural Areas was enacted (the new Basic Agriculture Law). In 2000, a part of the Agricultural Land Law was revised to promote agricultural enterprises. Although there were restrictions, it opened the doors for private corporations to enter the agriculture industry for the first time since the end of the war.

The new direction of the Ministry of Agriculture, the easing and abolition of price and distribution control, and the promotion of agricultural enterprises is appropriate. However, this policy change is only halfhearted, as the move toward independent farms and basic control continues.

Even though one part of the Agricultural Land Law was revised, the previously mentioned objectives set forth in article 1 have not been changed. In other words, agriculture policy is still for farmers who own their own land and any increase in agricultural productivity is pursued within (in fact, only within) the confines of what is feasible while also "stabilizing the position of the farmer."[11] I am not suggesting revival of the tenant farmer system or restoration of the colonial plantation system. However, a system is needed whereby normal agricultural corporate activities are possible. In the manufacturing industry ensuring the security of workers' pensions and positions does not mean that stockholders or management are severely restricted in terms of managing the company. The same idea should be applied to agriculture in restructuring the system, if agriculture is to be thought of as an industry.

Under the current Food Supply Law, market principles were to have been introduced and agricultural productivity was to have been increased. Instead, when the price of rice dramatically fell, the difference was made up by the Rice Stabilization Management Measure, which according to the Diet was a "temporary emergency response." The drop in price was due to the structural surplus in the supply of rice. By shifting the production from

11. Agricultural Land Law (my translation).

rice to other products, for the first time, it should have been possible to increase agricultural productivity. Instead, the income subsidy was increased for political reasons and the whole process that would have increased productivity was nullified. The largest problem concerning rice is that, in spite of the structural changes on the demand side because of variations in the population's diet, the supply side has not changed. Even though the Food Control Law was finally repealed and a new food supply law has been enacted, the income subsidy is still strongly entrenched and the actions taken have not changed the situation much from what it was before.

Before market mechanisms and agricultural corporate entities could be introduced into the market, pork barrel politics and the socialistic and cooperative administration had joined forces. Meanwhile, rapid depopulation continues in farming and fishing villages along with an exodus from the agriculture industry. While both the increase in independent farms and the maintenance of the natural habitat are important, are not such things possible only with the revitalization of agriculture as an industry? In order to achieve this, agricultural administrative regulations need to be loosened, creating an environment in which companies can freely conduct agriculture business. Additionally, excessive income subsidies and pork barrel politics should cease, and a market created to allow the price mechanism to work.

11 | Health Care Reform

U ntil recently, the debate regarding the Japanese health care industry centered on the health insurance problem and the policy response with regard to its deficit. For example, a recent white paper on public health stated the following about the reality and problems for the Japanese health care system: "In recent years, in the context of increasing medical costs due to the rapidly increasing number of elderly people, medical industry finances have gone into deficit, and in spite of the improvement resulting from the revision in the Medical Insurance Law in 1997, the situation continues to be serious."[1] In 1996, health care expenditures amounted to 8 percent of GDP and 4 percent of labor was employed in the sector. Since health care is an industry that will grow with the rapidly aging population, these percentages will only increase.

In essence, under the highly egalitarian and socialistic system of universal health insurance, problems are appearing in health care finance because of the rapid aging of

1. Ministry of Public Health, *Kōsei Hakusho Hēsē Jyūninenban* (Tokyo: Gyōsei, 2000), p. 189 (my translation).

Japan's population and the resulting increase in health care costs. The Ministry of Public Welfare and Labor is focusing attention on the medical insurance system and the financial deficit problem, rather than on health care as an industry. This may be natural for the ministry, which has bureaucratically maintained a socialistic policy. The health insurance system will collapse, however, if this policy continues. If, however, the health care industry were thought of as part of the services sector, its size would be close to that of the automotive industry. And if one takes into account the rapid aging of society, the medical industry has extremely promising prospects for growth.

History of Universal Health Care

To understand how the present socialistic health care system developed, a brief review of its history is necessary. Similar to many of the current systems in the Japanese economy and society, the medical insurance system was also born during the Taisho and Showa periods, partially established during the war, reformed in the postwar period, and nearly completed during the high-growth period. For details of the system's history, I refer the reader to a work by Kenji Yoshihara, who entered the Ministry of Health at the beginning of the high-growth period in 1955 and eventually became the Deputy Minister of Health, entitled the *History of the Japanese Medical Insurance System.*[2] The following is a brief look at the history.

The health insurance law was enacted in 1922 and implemented in 1926 for workers in mines and factories that employed more than 15 people. The implementation was delayed because of the Great Kanto Earthquake. Its launch was beset with complaints and dissatisfaction and its repeal was even discussed.[3] In Japan, where the influence of classical capitalism was still strong, it was difficult for the concept of universal health insurance to be accepted.

With the collapse of the classical capitalist system during the depression and war, however, the Universal Health Insurance Law was proposed in 1934 under the leadership of the progressive bureaucrats in the Social Bureau of the Ministry of the Interior. As an extremely progressive policy,

---

2. Kenji Yoshihara and Masaharu Wada, *Nihon no Iryōhokensēdo Shi* (Tokyo: Tōyō Kēzai Shinbun, 1999).

3. Japan, Ministry of Health and Welfare, *The Medical Insurance System of the 21st Century: The Direction of Fundamental Reform in Medical Insurance and in the Provision of Medical Care* (Tokyo, 1997), p. 1 (my translation).

this proposal caused a great sensation and stirred much debate. It was finally enacted in 1938 as a wartime measure to maintain national mobilization of all resources for the war effort. In the same year, at the request of the Ministry of the Army, the Public Health Ministry was made independent of the Ministry of the Interior. It became the prototype for the postwar Ministry of Public Health and the current Ministry of Health, Labor, and Welfare.

The current health care administration system and the health insurance system were, for the most part, established from around 1955 to 1975 during the high-growth period. As previously mentioned, during this final period of modernization in Japan, significant structural reforms were supported, on one hand, by the stabilization of employment and income in farm villages through the establishment of the public construction state system and, on the other hand, through the creation of safety nets in the form of a universal pension system and universal insurance. It was because of these safety nets and the employment and income stabilization that such significant structural reforms could be implemented without massive social and political upheaval. It is a fact that social work professionals like Yoshihara fought and cooperated with *zoku* politicians to create and maintain the universal pension and insurance systems and their accompanying structural reforms that supported the high growth of the Japanese economy, and they should be appreciated for it.

I have previously called the postwar Japanese capitalist system the "total war economic system."[4] The precursor to Japan's health insurance system and its directing ministry, the Ministry of Health, Labor, and Welfare, was also formed with that purpose in mind. This total war system is the prototype of the systems I call socialistic. Although this system of control still exists, there have been some changes. In the 1960s the Ministry of International Trade and Industry (currently the Ministry of Economy, Trade, and Industry) liberalized controls on trade and industry, as was the case with the administration of finances under the Ministry of Finance in the 1990s.

By 1959, the Citizens' Health Care Law, which was passed originally in 1938, was completely revised and the New Citizens' Health Insurance Law

4. Eisuke Sakakibara and Yukio Noguchi, "Ōkurashō, Nichigin Ōchō no Bunseki—Sōryokusenkē-zaitaisē no Shūen," *Chūokōron* (August 1977), pp. 6–7; Yukio Noguchi, *1940 nen Taisē* (Tokyo: Tōyō Kēzai Shinbunsha, 1995).

was enacted. The most important aspect of the law was the introduction of universal health insurance. Because the law established a complicated system and because the differences in each insurer's financial situation were taken into consideration, a grace period was allowed for its implementation. As a result, universal health insurance was not finally implemented until 1974, almost at the end of the high-growth period.

Partial Success of the Socialistic Health Care System

Because of the public good nature of health care, it is not fair to say that the system had problems because it was socialistic. If government is efficient, balances the competition between gainers and losers, and delivers good quality health care within certain financial constraints, then there is no need, ideologically, to criticize a policy for being socialistic.

In fact, the performance of the Japanese health care system was quite successful from the high-growth period through the 1990s. As is well known, the average life expectancy in Japan is the highest among that of developed nations. In 1960, the life expectancy for a 40-year-old man in Japan was 73 years on average, while in the United States and Germany it was 74 years. By the end of the high-growth period in 1975, however, this indicator for Japan surpassed that of other countries, reaching 76 years, versus 75 years in Germany and less than 75 years in the United States. By 1997, it had further increased to 81 years in Japan versus 78 years in Germany and the United States.

Of course, life expectancy is not determined solely by the health care system or medical services and, in the case of Japan, other factors such as food and life-style play a more than insignificant role. However, at least poor quality medical service or lack of availability of care does not appear to have reduced life expectancy. Furthermore, as is shown in table 11-1, this achievement of Japan's health care system has been accomplished at lower cost and with fewer medical service employees relative to GDP and total employment, respectively, than some other industrial countries.

However, in the 1990s, the relatively high performance of this system began to deteriorate. Figure 11-1 shows that the cost of national health care rose over the decade 1991–2001 by over 40 percent. Reflecting the aging of the Japanese population, the cost of medical care for senior citizens increased as a percentage of total medical care by an additional ten percentage points over the decade (1990–2000).

Table 11-1. *Medical Costs and Employment in Medical Services, Selected Countries, 1996*

Country	Cost of medical care as a percentage of GDP	Medical employment as percentage of total
United States	14	8
Germany	11	7
Japan	8	4
United Kingdom	7	5

Source: Compiled from McKinsey Global Institute, *Why the Japanese Economy Is Not Growing: Micro Barriers to Productivity Growth* (Washington, 2000), p. 50.

If this continues, it will eventually reach the higher levels of GDP of the United States and Germany and it is possible that deficits in insurance will mushroom. By 2000, national health insurance and cooperative health insurance had a cash flow shortage of ¥300 billion and debt of ¥200 billion, respectively. The government employee health insurance program is in the worst condition with a cash flow shortage of ¥600 billion. If this continues, by 2003 the accumulated funds will disappear.

In addition to the financial deterioration of the system, there is increasing dissatisfaction among citizens over the quality of medical care. Figure 11-2, which is from the McKinsey report cited in table 11-1, shows that among the five countries studied, patient satisfaction was lowest in Japan. While dissatisfaction over waiting times is particularly high, it is also troublesome that satisfaction with the quality of medical care is only 62 percent while it is 80 percent or more in the other four countries. From the same report, table 11-2 shows that along with waiting time, another major reason for dissatisfaction is the lack of explanation of examination results by the doctor. This attitude is consistent with the strong public demand for transparency and accountability in public services as a whole.

Moreover, as medical services expand with the aging of the population, the issues of rising medical costs, increasing deficits, and patient dissatisfaction are particularly serious problems. Gradual improvements in policy are no longer sufficient. Reform is drastically needed. Fortunately, the government is currently undertaking fundamental reforms, but progress seems too slow.

Figure 11-1. *Cost of Medical Care in Japan*[a]

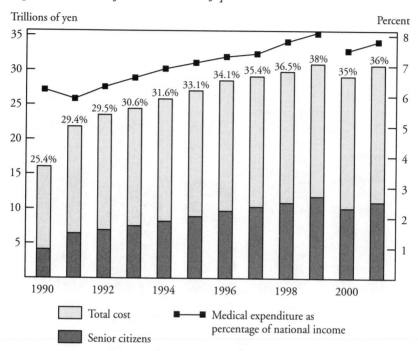

Total cost
Senior citizens
Medical expenditure as percentage of national income

Source: Compiled from Ministry of Finance data.

a. Data for 1999 are estimates; data for 2000 and 2001 are budget figures. Percentages shown above the bars indicate the share of medical care for senior citizens in total medical care costs.

Price Flexibility and Choice of Provider

In August 1997 the former Ministry of Health and Welfare (now the Ministry of Health, Labor, and Welfare) published a report on the future of the health care system, and submitted it to the opposition party's Health Insurance System Reform Discussion Group. Since then, medical reform has become one of the pillars of structural reform under the Koizumi government. The goal of reform, as stated at the beginning of the report, is to reduce the fiscal deficit that continues to grow as a result of "the rapidly aging population and the increases in medical costs due to such factors as the high level of treatment, the shift in the foundation of the economy, and the imbalance between the increase in medical costs and economic growth."[5]

5. Ministry of Health and Welfare, *The Medical Insurance System of the 21st Century*, p. 1.

Figure 11-2. *Results of International Survey on Patient Satisfaction*[a]

Percent of all respondents

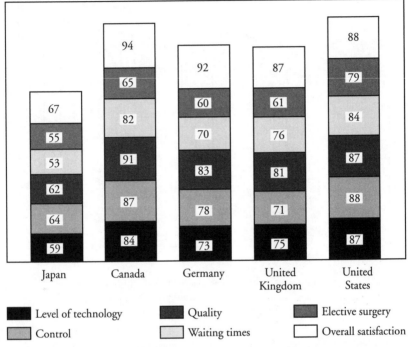

Source: McKinsey, *Why the Japanese Economy Is Not Growing*, "Health Care" section, Exhibit 3, p. 52.

a. Terms are defined as follows: *level of technology* = being able to get the most advanced tests, drugs, medical procedures, and equipment; *control* = having enough personal control over decisions affecting your own medical care; *quality* = receiving health care of the best possible quality; *waiting times* = not having to wait too long to get an appointment to see the doctor; *elective surgery* = being able to get elective surgery promptly without much delay; *overall satisfaction* = overall satisfaction with the health care available to you and members of your household.

What the report does not address is the extent to which the market should be involved in the health care system and how to balance equality and efficiency within the system. Of course, because of the nature of health care as a public good, it is out of the question to leave all aspects of the system to market mechanisms. It is probably even appropriate to maintain universal health insurance. However, if supply continues to be regulated as before and competition is controlled, no matter how much the insurance

Table 11-2. *Results of Domestic Patient Satisfaction Surveys*
Percent of all respondents

Reason for dissatisfaction	1998	1997	1996	1995	1994
Waiting time too long	45.9	47.2	43.6	45.1	40.5
Lack of explanation	44.8	44.0	47.1	45.9	44.1
Unkind doctors and nurses	21.6	22.2	19.3	18.1	21.6
Little communication with doctors and nurses	15.9	13.3	13.8	16.0	14.0
Confusing diagnosis	14.3	12.1	12.0	14.2	14.6

Source: McKinsey, *Why the Japanese Economy Is Not Growing*, "Health Care" section, Exhibit 4, p. 52.

system is manipulated the problems of the health care system, including that of financial deficit, will not be resolved.

From the viewpoint of deregulation and the introduction of market mechanisms, the primary issue is the price of medical care. At present it is almost completely set by the government because of the fee-for-service system. If the government fixes the fee, the market mechanism cannot function effectively. Although it might be appropriate to set the fee for a basic service or product, higher value-added treatments are a different matter. Information may not be equally available to the patient, the doctor, and the universal health care system. In these cases doctors, who have the greatest access to required information, should be allowed to set the fee. In a sense, this would be a mixed-fee system, except in the case of pricing for some dental procedures and for hospital beds; this has not yet been liberalized. The partial liberalization of fees is one of the pillars of an efficient health care system.

Along with price flexibility, patients and health insurance associations should be given freedom of choice.[6] In Japan, patients can choose a hospital but they cannot choose a health insurance association. It would not occur to many Japanese to choose their health insurance association. It is

6. In Japan's health care system, universal health coverage is provided via a multipayor insurance system. This system consists of 5,000 separate payors. National and local governments manage the insurance funds for over half the population (for example, for small firm employees, farmers, and retired people), while the rest of the population is covered by health insurance associations (also called insurance societies and mutual aid associations). These are often managed by an affiliated company or ministry. McKinsey Global Institute, *Why the Japanese Economy Is Not Growing: Micro Barriers to Productivity Growth* (Washington, 2000), pp. 3–4.

forbidden for the associations to choose hospitals (in other words, to determine the hospitals that members can go to for care) or for them to negotiate with hospitals on the price of care. Price flexibility and freedom of choice are prerequisites if some type of market mechanism is to be implemented.

If price flexibility and freedom of choice are allowed, adequate information should be made available to each individual on the quality of care and its price; otherwise, the market mechanism could work in a negative way. To make sure this does not happen, hospitals and doctors should be compelled to divulge information they possess. The complete disclosure of medical charts and invoices is a prerequisite to the implementation of such a measure. While it is obvious that for privacy purposes patient approval should be sought before giving others access to such information, in other cases all information should be disclosed.

In addition to the disclosure of information, it is necessary to establish a reliable system of evaluation. Naohiro Yashiro and the Ministry of Economy, Trade, and Industry group rightly point out the importance of creating a system of third-party evaluation that includes patients and insurers (the health insurance associations).[7] Also important are reforming the regulation related to advertising and providing the option of a second opinion.

Despite the strong tendency of the Japan Doctors Association and the Japan Dentists Association to oppose the promotion of competition and the introduction of market mechanisms, the government should resolutely move forward, particularly on the issues of disclosure and evaluation where sufficient public support already exists.

Another problem is that as payors, the health insurance associations have in part become administrative organs and have not played enough of a role in promoting the disclosure of information or in promoting competition. Health insurance associations should be on the demand side by being allowed to engage in private sector activities, such as the negotiation of price with medical institutions. Furthermore, if the insured were allowed to choose associations, the activities of health insurance associations would be revitalized. The entrance of private corporations into hospital management and the corporate management of health insurance associations are

7. Naohiro Yashiro, *Kaikaku Shidō suru Nihon no Iryō Service* (Tokyo: Tōyō Keizai Shinpōsha, 1999).

extremely important pillars of reform in that they will promote the efficiency of the health care system.

The government should be praised for actively trying to use private sector vitality and principles of competition to strengthen the role of the insurers and to disclose information. However, if this is being done only to reduce the financial deficit so that the old system can be maintained, that is not sufficient. The socialistic system, which was created under the wartime structure, needs to be fundamentally reformed. For that, the old iron triangle of politicians, government, and vested interests must be dismantled and, in its place, a transparent and open system must be built. The reduction in financial deficit will be the result of such measures.

The market is not a cure-all. It is not necessary to choose between regulation and liberalization. The challenge is rather to apply each where it will produce the desired goals of containing cost and improving the quality of care.

12 | Building a New Nation

The terrorist attacks in the United States on September 11, 2001, occurred while I was writing this book. Since then, I have reread the book to see if anything needed to be revised. I found that everything I had written was still applicable, because the recent terrorist attacks and "war" are incorporated into the phenomenon of the great collapse and transformation that I refer to in chapter 1.

First, it should be stated clearly that the terrorist attacks that have been perpetrated by Osama bin Laden, al Qaeda, and the fundamentalist cells of the Mujahadeen are hateful crimes. Having stated that, it is ironic and worth noting that those actions were the result of the skillful use of globalization by the nonglobalization movement. It was a backlash against the globalization elite by a minority (albeit criminal) global network. Though their ideology is that of antiglobalization, they are an element of the fallout from the collapse under network globalization. In other words, this crime has been committed in the process of transformation from hierarchical globalization to network globalization.

Although there have been intermittent local wars on the Korean Penin-sula, in the Middle East, and in Vietnam, the world as a whole has generally been peaceful since World War II. And with the end of the cold war, the United States and the world reached a peak of prosperity in the 1990s under *Pax Americana*. From 1993 to 2000 average real GDP growth in the United States was 4 percent, and the unemployment rate in 2000 was the lowest in five years: 3.9 percent. In spite of the low unemployment rate, core inflation has remained around 2–3 percent, due to the increase in productivity. While the average increase in labor productivity from 1973 to 1995 is estimated to have been around 1.4 percent, from 1995 to 1999 that productivity is thought to have increased approximately 1 percent, to an annual average of 2.5 percent. Some economists thought this increase in productivity was the result of cyclical improvement in the economy. Many, including Alan Greenspan, thought, however, that it was because of the change in the struc-ture of the economy resulting from the information technology revolution.[1]

Significance of September 11

The terrorist attacks of 9/11 occurred just as the optimistic outlook for eco-nomic growth and the increase in productivity began to decline with the collapsing of the information technology bubble and the stock market bub-ble. It was not certain if the U.S. economy would aggressively bounce back beginning in 2002 or whether it would enter a mid- to long-term period of stagnation. Because the economic fundamentals are still strong and because the U.S. military and the U.S. economy are so powerful worldwide, it is hard to imagine that U.S. hegemony would collapse easily. Nevertheless, the excessive optimism and enthusiasm for globalization and the information technology revolution have unmistakably diminished, and the process of the collapse of the previous era and the transformation into a new era will cer-tainly not be without problems. U.S. hegemony will probably continue, at least for a while longer. Depending on the progress of this war on terrorism, however, we may be seeing the beginning of the end of *Pax Americana*.

Just after the attacks, Thomas Friedman, a columnist for the *New York Times*, stated on television that "this was the beginning of World War III."[2]

1. Robert J. Gordon, "Does the 'New Economy' Measure Up to the Great Inventions of the Past," Working Paper 7833 (Cambridge, Mass.: National Bureau for Economic Research, 2000).
2. CNN, September 13, 2001.

This is a typically journalistic expression, characterized by exaggeration and metaphor. Nevertheless, this war will not be at all like World War I or World War II. It is very unlikely that nuclear weapons or intercontinental ballistic missiles will be used. What the United States, or rather the terrorists, started is clearly a "war," and is fundamentally different from the previous incidents of terrorism and retaliation. It is also certain that, unlike previous wars that were fought between sovereign nations, this is a global war that spans national borders. Although this war may not become a world war in the same sense as those of the previous century, it is certain to be a new, twenty-first-century war. The continuation of peace for more than fifty years is historically unusual. It would not be surprising if, as a result of this incident, the long period of peace came to an end. One should keep in mind that this instability is occurring at a time when the world is already going through major collapse and transformation.

It is interesting to note that the era of *Pax Britannica* was also a time of information revolution and globalization (for example, telephone, telegraph, and airplanes). Even though that was different in nature from the current information revolution and globalization, it is a curious historical coincidence that it was also brought to an end by war.

In the twentieth century, the newly developed networks or the technological progress that supported globalization did not break down; it is unlikely to do so during this century. Nevertheless, it is certain that the war will dramatically alter politics and economics and speed up the process of change. I do not know what kind of world will emerge from this collapse and transformation; however, I am almost certain the twenty-first century will be characterized by a postmodern system that is completely different from that of the two centuries preceding it.

Past Success and Present Decay of an Affluent Society

Except for city-states, such as Singapore and Hong Kong, Japan was the only non-Western country to succeed at modernization and industrialization. India and China, which in premodern times had led the world, stagnated in the eighteenth and nineteenth centuries, were colonized, then became socialist. Japan, at least in terms of its economy, became one of the world's leading countries in spite of World War II and defeat.

It is true that behind Japan's successful modernization were progressive elements of the modern world that dated from as far back as the Edo period, which were typified by the agricultural revolution. However, the fact that it was Japan, and not China with its similarly long history and progressive elements, that succeeded in modernization deserves attention. Japanese modernization and industrialization have already been addressed in chapter 2, so there is no need to repeat it here. What is important to note is that it was the high-growth process that completed Japan's industrialization and resulted in the establishment of the structures of Japanese capitalism. During the development of the Asian economy in the 1980s, this model of Japanese capitalism captured the attention of key officials in the governments of East Asia and Southeast Asia.

Unfortunately, success is the greatest cause of failure. While in the past the brilliant success of high growth and the realization of the Japanese miracle made Japan as wealthy as, or even more wealthy than, other developed nations, now that affluence is causing Japan many very difficult problems. Many Japanese do not like to admit that Japan is one of the world's wealthiest countries; however, in 1999, at $35,517 Japan's per capita GDP was the highest among G-7 countries. That figure was $200 more than that of the United States, where there had been continued high growth during the 1990s. In 1999, per capita GDP was $33,836 in the United States, $23,912 in France, and $24,228 in the United Kingdom.

Because prices are high in Japan, the per capita GDP numbers need to be adjusted somewhat in terms of purchasing power. On the other hand, because income distribution is remarkably equal in Japan, the figures should be for the most part adjusted upward with regard to the average citizen's income. In any case, average citizens in Japan enjoy some of the highest levels of wealth in the world.

Despite ten years of low growth and economic stagnation, past success and current wealth still allow many Japanese to feel somewhat satisfied, which has become an obstacle to drastically changing the current situation. I completely agree with the *Financial Times* journalist who recently called the last ten years of stagnation in Japan the "golden recession" and claimed that the structural problem in Japan is that the Japanese people are lacking a sense of crisis.[3] This is the negative result of past success and present wealth.

Nevertheless, the world's great transformation is putting significant pressure on Japan to carry out structural reform, whether Japan recognizes it or not. The Japanese structures that have not yet been reformed are decaying. In response to long-term stagnation, the government used fiscal policy to

3. Daniel Bogler, "The Golden Recession," *Euro Japanese Journal* (Spring 2001).

stimulate the economy while corporations tolerated excess employment. In the political and economic systems that I have called socialistic, it is natural to use such safety nets as a means to avoid or delay the negative effects on individuals of the reversal of the economy. That might be an appropriate policy if the stagnation of the economy were just cyclical. If the problems were not structural, Japan's macro policy and the private sector response to stagnation as a whole would have been more or less appropriate.

Unfortunately, the problems Japan has faced for the last ten years or so have been structural rather than cyclical and cannot be dealt with through Keynesian fiscal policy or through Japanese-style management techniques dating from the high-growth period. In fact, proceeding along these lines has deepened the problem. Japan's fiscal situation has rapidly grown worse as outlined in chapter 4. The reason the problems are not worse is because the saving rate is high in Japan and individuals and corporations own the majority of government bonds. However, the deterioration of the government's fiscal structure lowers the quality of national and local bonds, which make up a significant portion of individual and corporate assets. By continuously using fiscal safety nets, the Japanese people are in fact reducing their own assets.

Because of declining stock prices that are due to poor corporate performance, and because of the increase in nonperforming loans held by banks, the value of individual assets is deteriorating, as previously pointed out. Even though there is a government safety net and bank principal is insured, in the end it will be the individual who has to pay. During the "golden recession" of the 1990s, individual real incomes still continued to rise on average (1.3 percent annually); and, in terms of the value of assets, there was yet no need to dip into the principal of government bonds or savings accounts. However, from the end of 2001 to 2002, the structural problems coincided with a worldwide recession, with the result that individuals were hurt as unemployment increased, savings dramatically shrank, and assets depreciated in real terms.

Japan, which had lived off its wealth until now, has finally reached a critical point. The problems, as noted above, are structural. This means that unless they are resolved, the recession will continue. Keynesian policies, such as public works and tax cuts, do not even have temporary benefits; they only serve to exacerbate the structural problems. And unless the nonperforming loan and excess employment problems are squarely confronted, the situation for the private sector will only get worse.

Japan is about to enter into crises of the economic, as well as of the political and social, systems to a degree that it has never before experienced. I cannot forget what Prime Minister Mahathir of Malaysia said to me when we had the opportunity to talk in October 2001 about the Asian, as well as Japanese, crisis: "About fifty years ago, Japan rose like a phoenix out of ruin. We saw that and made our slogan 'Look East.' What is important at a time of crisis is to return to the basics. I would like Japan and the Japanese to return to the basics."[4]

Institutional Reform for the New Japan

Returning to the basics means that we need a new vision for our nation—a vision of a new social system and a new economic system. To achieve this we need to aggressively pursue systemic reform. It is certainly not easy to find and confidently demonstrate a clear vision during a time of great transformation.

As discussed in chapter 4, the problems of the current system are quite clear in each area. It is true that, unlike during the Meiji Restoration or after World War II, when Japan could look to the United Kingdom or the United States for models, none exists today for Japan. However, if we think about it, this is rather natural. Visualizing a new nation will only be possible based on an understanding of the current changes in the environment and the particular historical developments in each field. The Japanese capitalist system, which was completed during the high-growth period, was not based on any previous model either. In a sense, it was the combination of Japanese culture, tradition, and systems from the Edo period and beyond that led to the post–Meiji Restoration reforms, the changes during the 1930s and 1940s, and the aggressive system building of the high-growth period. Although legal structures and systems of some countries were used as models, it was only natural that the end product was uniquely Japanese. It should be the same for the structural and systemic reforms that are needed now. There may be areas we might borrow from the United States or Korea. The system that will be created, however, will naturally be Japanese. Systems that are not adapted to Japan will not work for Japan.

The reforms needed to create a new Japan will take a long time, perhaps five to ten years. We should keep in mind that it took fifteen to twenty

4. Mohamad Mahathir, interview by Eisuke Sakakibara, October 2001.

years to complete the systems necessary for the high-growth process. Japan's modernization and industrialization took more than 100 years. It is a mistake to think that structural reform will take only one or two years. Just to change a law normally takes three years, from the beginning of the revision to the time the new law is implemented. One of the laws that I was personally involved in revising, the Foreign Exchange and Foreign Trade Law, was first put on the agenda for revision by the Foreign Exchange Commission on November 2, 1995, and the revised law was finally made effective on April 1, 1998. Although I thought we had worked with incredible speed, it still took two and a half years.

For the systemic reform necessary to build a new nation, the constitution plus several hundred laws need to be changed. While many of these revisions can proceed simultaneously, it clearly cannot be accomplished in the short term. It could take anywhere from five to ten years. If the course of reform were to zigzag, it could take twenty or thirty years. Moreover, this has to take place during worldwide transformation.[5]

Many Japanese are accustomed to living in peace, or rather deluded because of having lived only during peaceful times. They think that it is possible to have structural reform and major systemic reform through policymaking before a crisis occurs, or even without having a real crisis. It is true that the postwar structural reforms were one of the few reforms that proceeded smoothly through the policymaking process. However, even this was made possible because of the postwar systemic reforms that came out of the catastrophe of World War II. It is ironic that the reforms that the elite and the intelligentsia wanted before the war became possible only after, and because of, World War II. Land liberalization and the dissolution of the *zaibatsu* are among such reforms.

In this way, the global recession that the world is currently entering into is really a prelude to systemic reform in Japan and around the world. In such an environment, Japanese structural and systemic reform may be accelerated. In no way does this mean that I am wishing for worldwide recession, depression, or a crisis. However, understanding historical dynamics makes it clear that crisis and reform are two sides of the same

5. It is clear from history that in most cases, large-scale reform comes about as the result of a major crisis. The opening of the Edo government required more than 100 years of turbulence, and the Meiji Restoration and its subsequent reforms required the threat of possible colonization. Even looking at the twentieth century, the large systemic reforms and changes took place as a result of World War I, the Great Depression, and World War II.

coin. It is because of crisis that reform is needed. If there is no crisis, the system does not need to be reformed.

Sometimes humans are powerless in the face of history. At such times, policymaking and systemic reform are meaningless. Through war and panic, systems are destroyed beyond the reach of policy. Because of this, it is dangerous to be overconfident about policy. Nevertheless, I am certain that the only choice we have is to accept the large tides of history, calmly analyze the situation, and continue to make small but significant efforts.

Index

Administrative reform, proposed, 40, 45
Agricultural Land Law, 131, 140
Agricultural sector: Edo period, 13, 14,
    23–24; employment statistics, 29,
    130, 133–35, 138; government
    subsidies, 42; high-growth period,
    18–19, 21, 29; and income-wage
    disparity, 42–43; irrigation projects,
    51–54; land ownership, 131, 133;
    price controls, 136, 139, 140–41;
    productivity levels, 129–30, 132;
    public budgets compared, 137–39;
    reform history, 77–78, 136–37, 140;
    reforms proposed, 140–41
Alcock, Sir Rutherford, 23
Allied Occupation, reform policies,
    60–61, 77–78, 89–90, 131
Amakawa, Akira, 112–13, 117
Aoki, Masahiko, xiii
Aonuma, Yoshimatsu, 59
Ashida, Hitoshi, 89–90
Attali, Jacques, 8–9
Ayukawa, Yoshisuke, 62

Banking sector: and corporate
    governance, 74–75; development,
    75–77; high-growth period, 20, 79;
    nonperforming loan levels, xiv–xvi,
    71–73; post–World War II reforms,
    77–79; reform needs, 83–86; shift in
    sector focus, 79–83; *zaibatsu*
    relationship, 62–63
Bank of Japan, viii, 62–63
Bank of Japan Act, 63
Basic Agriculture Law, 135–36
Basic Education Law, 106–07
Battle of Sea of Japan, 16–17
Birthrates, 94
Braudel, Fernand, 39
Bribery, 48, 50
Britain. *See* United Kingdom
Budget policymaking, party
    involvement, 49–50

Canada, xv, 3, 113
Capital gains taxes, 46
Capitalism, Japanese, 39–41

Capitalization: classical globalization era, 3; retail industry loan guarantees, 46, 50–51. *See also* Banking sector; Corporate system; Public works investment

Central-local government relationships: irrigation projects, 50–51; models of, 15–16, 111–13, 116–17; and party politics, 113, 117–18; proposed reforms, 125–28; and small business entry/exit barriers, 45–46; spending levels compared, 35, 113–16, 118–19, 121–25

Charter schools, 108–09

China, x, xv–xvi, 13

Colonization era, 12–13

Construction industry: employment statistics, x, 29, 134; high-growth period, 21; irrigation projects, 53; productivity, ix–x, 36–37; public finance structure, 29–35, 118–19, 121–22. *See also* Public works investment

Corporate earnings, ix

Corporate system: as engine of high-growth period, 20–21; Ghosn-based reforms, 67–69; *keiretsu* competition, 21, 64–68; *zaibatsu* companies, 59–64. *See also* Banking sector

Council for Fiscal and Economic Affairs, 49

Council for Policy Coordination, 49

Cross-stockholding, 62, 78–79, 81–82

Curriculum needs, 104–05, 106

Dan, Takuma, 60, 62

Debt levels: agricultural households, 43, 137; summarized, xiv–xv, 71–73

Deflation, xv–xvi

Democracy: and globalization, 1–2, 4, 7–9; policymaking process, 55–56

Democratic Party, remilitarization policy, 89–90

Diplomacy structure, proposed changes, 98–100

Domestic sector: as banking sector focus, 80; employment statistics, 134; productivity differentials, ix, 44–47; retail industry, 45–46, 50–51. *See also* Agricultural sector; Health care industry

Dulles, John Foster, 89

Economic system as dual structure, 41–47: interaction with political system, 50–51; proposed reform, 40

Edo period, 13–16, 23–24, 87–89, 129–30

Educational exchange system, 93

Education system: development, 101–02; diminishing value, 102–05; and foreign policy reform, 99; proposed reforms, 40–41, 105–10

Emergency Rescue Plan, 26

Employment statistics: agriculture, 29, 130, 133–35, 138; construction industry, x, 29, 134; and dual economic structure, 42; health care industry, 142; high-growth period, 18, 19, 21; manufacturing sector, x, 18, 44, 134; and productivity levels, 44–45; sectors compared, 44–45, 134

Entry and exit barriers, 45–46, 50

European Union, 7–9, 47, 93

Export-oriented manufacturing, x, 42, 44, 47. *See also* Corporate system

Fan, Gang, xvi

Farmland Adjustment Law, 131

Farm sector. *See* Agricultural sector

Financial Services Agency (FSA), xi

Fisheries sector, 26, 137–39

Food Control Law, 131, 136, 139
Food Supply Law, 140–41
Foreign Exchange and Foreign Trade
  Law, 158
Foreign policy regime: cold war
  isolationism, 90–93, 95; isolationist
  heritage, 87–89; proposed reforms,
  95–100; remilitarization issue, 89–91
Forestries sector, 21, 26, 137–39
Fortune, Robert, 24
France, xv, 45, 138, 155
Frank, Andre Gunder, 96
Free trade system, 12–14, 16–18
Friedman, Thomas, 5–6, 153
Fukuyama, Francis, 5, 6–7
Fukuzawa, Yukichi, 16, 17

General Council, 49
General Headquarters, reform policies,
  60–61, 77–78, 89–90, 131
Germany: banking sector, 75; deflation,
  xv; life expectancy, 145; public works
  expenditures, 35, 113
Ghosn, Carlos, 67–68
Globalization: classical, 2–5; and
  corporate system reforms, 67–69; and
  deflation, xv–xvi; eras compared, 2–7;
  and European Union path, 7–9;
  hierarchical, 6; ideological arguments,
  1–2; and immigration, 93–95;
  neoclassical, 2–5; network, 5–9; as
  reform motive, xii–xiii; and terrorist
  attacks, 152, 153–54
Gotō, Yonosuke, 41
Guéhenno, Jean-Marie, 2

Hara, Kei, 25–26, 35
Hara, Yonosuke, 13
Hata, Makoto, 133, 135
Hatoyama, Ichiro, 90
Hausbank, 75

Hayami, Akira, 13
Hayashi, Senjurô, 62
Health care industry: citizen satisfaction,
  146; demographics and, 142–43;
  expenditures, 142, 145–47; historical
  overview, 143–45; proposed reforms,
  147–51
High-growth period: banking sector
  influence, 20, 79; construction state
  development, 29–36; health care
  industry, 144–45; and remilitarization
  issue, 91; summarized, 18–22
Hitachi Manufacturing, 63
Horizontal revolution, 67, 68–69
Hübner, Joseph Alexander von, 16

Ikeda, Shigeaki, 60, 62
Immigration policy, 40–41, 93–95
Income levels, ix, 42–43, 136–37, 155,
  156
India, 17–18
Industrial Bank of Japan (IBJ), 62–63,
  77
Industrialization. *See* Modernization
  history
Information flow: after World War II,
  91–93; Edo period, 88–89; proposed
  changes, 98–100
Information technology. *See*
  Technological innovations
Infrastructure investment. *See* Public
  works investment
Inheritance taxes, 46
Institutions, as structure, xi–xii
Interfusion vs. separation, government
  relationships, 112–13, 116–17
International Monetary Fund, 10
Investment demand and stagnation,
  viii–x
Iron triangle, defined, xi
Irrigation projects, 51–53

IS curve (investment-saving), viii–ix
Isolationist policy: immigration, 41,
    93–95; and information flow, 91–93;
    proposed reforms, 95–100; tradition
    of, 13–14, 16–18, 87–89
Itami, Hiroyuki, 64
Ito, Hirofumi, 102
Japan Development Bank, 51

Kawakatsu, Heita, 17
Keidanren, 79, 90
Keiretsu system, 21, 64–69
Keynes, John Maynard, 2–4
Kido, Takayoshi, 16
Kishimoto, Mutsuhisa, 108
Koizumi government, xiii, 37, 49
Krugman, Paul, vii

Land ownership, 131, 133
Large-Scale Retail Location Law, 45–46
LAT system, 117, 122–24, 126–28
Lemierre, Jean, 9
Liberal Democratic Party (LDP), xi, xiii,
    47, 51, 52, 90, 139
Liberal Party, remilitarization policy, 90
Life expectancy, 145
LM curve (liquidity-money), viii–ix
Loan guarantees, 46, 50–51
Loans, nonperforming, xiv–xvi, 71–73
Loan syndicates, 63, 76–77
Local Allocation Tax system, 117,
    122–24, 126–28
Local governments. *See* Central-local
    government relationships

Mahathir bin Mohamad, 157
Management Bureau, 52–53
Manufacturing sector: employment
    statistics, x, 18, 44, 134; high-growth
    period, 21; productivity differentials,
    42, 43, 44. *See also* Corporate system

Media. *See* Information flow
Meiji government, 15–16, 25, 101–02
Meritocracy system: development, 16,
    101–02; diminishing importance,
    102–04. *See also* Education system
Military industry: financing/spending,
    60–61, 76–77, 88; and high-growth
    period, 20–21
Ministry of Agriculture, Forestry, and
    Fisheries (MAFF), 51–53, 135–36,
    137–38
Ministry of Economy, Trade, and
    Industry, xi
Ministry of Education and Science,
    40–41, 103, 104–05, 106, 109
Ministry of Finance, xi, 49, 117
Ministry of Foreign Affairs, 91–92, 96,
    98–99
Ministry of Health, Labor, and Welfare,
    144
Ministry of Home Affairs, 117
Ministry of International Trade and
    Industry (MITI), 50–51
Ministry of Munitions, 76–77
Ministry of Public Welfare and Labor,
    143
Ministry of the Interior, 112, 116–17,
    143–44
Mitani, Taichirō, 25
Mitsubishi, 68–69
Mitsui, 59, 60, 62
Modernization history: before World
    War II, 12–18, 26, 75–77; destructive
    effects, 23–25, 29; high-growth
    period, 18–22. *See also* Corporate
    system
Mori, Arinori, 102
Mori, Satoru, 62
Morikawa, Hidemasa, 59, 62
Multilateralism, 8–9
Muramatsu, Michio, 112, 113

Nagasu, Kazuji, 41–42
Najita, Tetsuo, 25
Nakajima, Chikuhei, 62
Nakajima Aircraft, 62, 63
Nakamigawa, Hikojirō, 59
Nakamura, Takafusa, 13, 20–21, 63
Nakane, Chie, 15
Nakano, Minoru, 118
Nakaumi Reclamation and Desalination
    Project, 53–54
Narita, Norihiko, 50
Naturalization restrictions, 94
New Citizens' Health Insurance Law,
    144–45
Nihon Densō, 67
Nissan Motors, 62, 63, 67
Noda, Nobuo, 1–2, 96–97
Nonperforming assets, xiv–xvi, 71–73.
    See also Banking sector

Oda, Nobunaga, 88
Oil Industry Law, 63–64
Ōishi, Shinzaburō, 88–89, 129, 130
Ōki, Takato, 101–02
Ono, Motoyuki, 106

Pacifism and information flow, 92–93
Parallel Partial Progression (PPP), xvi
Party politics: agricultural sector,
    52–54, 139; and decentralized
    government, 113, 117–18;
    policymaking power, 47–50, 54–56;
    as reform motive, xi–xii; in retail loan
    guarantees, 50–51; Taisho period,
    25–26
Pax Americana, 89, 153
Pax Britannica, 2–5, 12, 18, 154
Pax Tokugawana, 88–89
Policymaking process: industrial
    influence, 63–64; party involvement,
    47–50, 55–56

Political system as dual structure: charac-
    teristics, 47–50; interaction with
    economic system, 50–54; and party-
    bureaucracy complex, 54–56;
    proposed reforms, 40, 45–46, 56–57
Population statistics, 18
Price regulation: agriculture, 136, 139,
    140–41; health care industry, 149
Prime ministers: ambassador
    appointments, 99; policymaking
    roles, 55–57
Productivity levels: agriculture, 42, 43,
    129–30, 132; construction industry,
    ix–x, 36–37; as dual structure
    characteristic, 42, 43–47; and
    immigration, 94–95; manufacturing
    sector, 42, 43, 44; public
    construction, 36–37; service sector, ix,
    44–45; United States, 44, 45, 153
Property taxes, 46
Provisional Council on Educational
    Reform, 103
Public corporations, 32–33
Public works investment: financial
    structure, 29–35, 113, 118–19,
    121–22, 127; historical overview,
    25–29; importance, 21–22, 35–36;
    productivity declines, 36–37; as rural
    support, 42, 43; tax legislation,
    29–32; and *zaibatsu* transformation,
    60–61

Railroads, 25–26, 27
Regional cooperation movement, 9–11
Remilitarization policy, 89–91
Retail industry, 45–46, 50–51
Rice Stabilization Management
    Measure, 140–41
Riken Science Industries, 63
Road Construction and Improvement
    Special Account, 32

Roads: public corporation development, 32–34; railroad investments compared, 26; spending levels, 26, 27–29, 33, 35; tax sources, 29–32. *See also* Public works investment

Rodrik, Dani, 4

Russo-Japanese War, 16–17

Satō, Tsuneo, 14, 130

Savings levels, 43, 156

School Education Law, 106–07

Schools. *See* Education system

Second Land Reform Bill, 131

Securities Adjustment Cooperative Committee, 78

Seiyūkai party, 25

Separation vs. interfusion, government relationships, 112–13, 116–17

September *11* attacks, 152, 153–54

Sheard, Paul, 74

Shiba, Ryōtarō, 16

Shimomura, Osamu, 19, 41

Shinohara, Miyohei, 42

Shōsha companies, 68–69

Showa Electric, 62

Small business: dual structure impact, 50–51; entry and exit barriers, 45–46

Soros, George, 4

South Korea, 10

Stagnation, viii–x

Stocks: and corporate governance, 75, 80; ownership changes, 75–76, 78–79, 81–82

Structural reform: difficulty of, xiii–xvi, 157–59; need for, viii–xiii, 155–57; types, 40–41

Structure, defined, xi–xii, 39–40

Sumitomo, 59

Taisho period, 25–26

Takahashi, Korekiyo, 26–27, 60–61

Takahashi Finance Plan, 60–61

Takeda, Katsuyori, 88

Tanaka, Akihiko, 1–2

Tanaka, Kakuei, 29, 32, 35

Tanaka period, 25–26

Taxes: as construction resources, 29–32; Edo period, 14; land, 131; local allocation, 117, 122–24, 126–27; as retail exit barrier, 46; Taisho period, 25

Technological innovations: and corporate system, 63–64, 67–69; and deflation, xv–xvi; globalization eras compared, 3–7; and high-growth period, 20–21; and immigration, 94–95; as reform motive, xii–xiii

Technology sharing, 64–69

Terrorist attacks, 152, 153–54

Textile industry, 17–18

Thailand, 10, 13

Toffler, Alvin, 5

Tokugawa, Ieyasu, 88–89

Town Center Revitalization Law, 46

Toyota Motors, 63, 67, 68

Trust Fund Bureau, 32, 63, 124

United Kingdom: agriculture sector, 138–39; classical globalization era, 2–3; immigration policy, 94; income levels, 155; policymaking process, 47–48, 50, 55; relations with *18*th century Japan, 12–14

United States: agriculture sector, 138–39; deflation, xv; free trade areas, 10; immigration policy, 94–95; income levels, 155; as information source, 91–93; life expectancy, 145; nonperforming assets, xiv; overseas investments, 3; post–World War II growth, 153; public works expenditures, 35, 113; service sector productivity, 44, 45; wages vs. corporate income, ix

Universal Health Insurance Law, 143–44
Urban Redevelopment Law, 46
U.S.-Japan Security Treaty, 89–90, 96

Vertical administrative control model, 112–13
Village system: Edo and Meiji periods compared, 15–16; and high-growth period changes, 21–22. *See also* Central-local government relationships

Wada, Hideki, 102–03
Wage-income disparity, ix, 41–43, 136–37

Watanabe, Kyōji, 18, 24, 29

Yashiro, Naohiro, 150
Yasuda, 59
Yazawa, Eiichi, 15
Yoshida, Shigeru, 90, 98
Yoshihara, Kenji, 143
Yoshitomi, Masaru, ix
Yūki, Toyotarō, 62

Zaibatsu companies, 20, 59–64, 75–76, 77–78, 79
Zoku politicians, 37, 50, 54–55